邮票上的

陈德芬 编著
陈 莉 翻译

西北大学出版社

Buddhist Pagodas Featured
On Postage Stamps

邮　　　票　　　上　　　的

作者简介

　　陈德芬，山东青岛人。毕业于北京大学，在教育系统工作多年，高级工程师。爱好古建筑特别是佛教古建筑方面的资料收集和研究。业余爱好集邮，曾主持编组"佛塔专题邮集"参加国内外邮展，并获"全国邮展镀金奖"和"泰国世界邮展大银奖"。

译者简介

　　陈莉，陕西西安人。毕业于西安外国语大学，文学硕士。长期从事高校英语教学与科研工作，副教授。曾参加"佛塔专题邮集"的编纂工作。

序言

佛塔高大、雄伟、端庄、秀丽，不论在何处，佛塔都是一处亮丽的风貌景观。

佛塔中最具影响力、具有代表性的著名佛塔，是佛塔中的佼佼者，是各国佛塔中的精华。它们有的列入世界文化遗产名录，有的定为一国的国宝或国家重点文物保护单位。

邮票是一个国家的名片，是一部小型的形象百科全书，它集中展现了一国或一地区各个方面的主要成就。

各国著名佛塔反映了当地的文化、宗教、民俗及建筑工艺等方面的重要成就，自然会入选为邮票图案。实际上各国已发行邮票上的佛塔，基本上囊括了世界上几乎所有著名的佛塔。

各国入选邮票的著名佛塔除少数外，本书均已收录。包含各国著名佛塔65座，其中中国著名佛塔27座，外国著名佛塔38座。

本书对这些佛塔的描述和介绍有所侧重。对中国佛塔的介绍，国内已有多部中文专著出版，且多以文字为主，本书则增录了佛塔图案的邮品和若干佛塔图片。对外国佛塔的介绍，目前中文专著不多，本书试图对外国的著名佛塔做一集中介绍。因条件所限，对一些外国佛塔的描述较为粗略。

外国佛塔的中文名称，通常是音译，翻译过来的塔名难免会出现差异。本书采用的塔名均选自《中华世界邮票目录》。书中选用的佛塔邮票，也以该目录为准。

本书为中英文对照版本。总论部分和各个佛塔的说明文字附有英文版本，为各国朋友参访和研究佛塔提供方便。

PREFACE

Pagodas, grand and elegant in appearance, can always offer spectacular views wherever they are. The most influential and representative pagodas are among the best ones and represent the quintessence of pagoda construction in the countries of the world. Some of them are listed in the *Chronology of Recognition of World Heritages* and some others are designated as national treasure or the important heritage site under state protection.

Stamps are, as they were, the calling cards of a country and the miniature of image encyclopedia, through which the features of a country or a region are displayed.

The construction of the famous pagodas can reflect the major achievements of a country in culture, religion, custom and architecture, and thus many of them have been chosen and presented in the stamps.

All the famous pagodas featured on postage stamps, with few exceptions, are included in the book, totaling 65 ancient Buddhist pagodas, among which 27 are pagodas in China, 38 in some other countries.

Particular emphasis is laid when these pagodas are described and introduced. For the pagodas in China, images of the structures and the postage stamps featuring them are offered in the book, since several other books written in Chinese have been published, most of them focusing on text description. Chinese books introducing pagodas of other countries are relatively few, and therefore, an overall introduction to those pagodas is included in the book.

The Chinese terms for the pagodas in foreign countries are usually transliterated and thus different versions of the names exist. The names adopted in the book are in correspondence with those in *Dragon World Stamp Catalogue*. The stamps featuring pagodas are also chosen from the *Catalogue*.

The book is written in both Chinese and English in order to help readers better understand and appreciate the beauty of Buddhist pagodas.

目录

邮票上的

佛塔

Buddhist Pagodas Featured On Postage Stamps

佛塔的
结构形态及其演变
Structural Form of Pagodas and Its Evolvement

　　佛塔是因佛教而产生的。当初佛祖释迦牟尼逝世后，弟子们将其遗体火化，得到若干舍利子，他们将佛舍利子和佛祖的其他遗骨遗物保存在类似坟冢的建筑物内，这种建筑物就是早期的佛塔。以后随着佛教的传播，佛塔这种建筑也扩散到亚洲各地。

　　历史上，佛教传播的路径基本有三条。一是从古印度传入斯里兰卡，并向东传入缅甸、泰国、老挝、柬埔寨和印度尼西亚等国，是为南传佛教。二是从古印度向北传入中亚，再向东传入中国，再传入朝鲜半岛、日本、越南等国家和地区，是为汉传佛教。三是从古印度传入中国西藏，再传入中国内地和蒙古国等地，是为藏传佛教。

　　各佛教传播区佛塔的形制有很大区别，各有其显著特点。南传佛教和藏传佛教地区多是单层塔，汉传佛教地区则是多层塔。

　　常见的大中型佛塔中，汉传佛教地区主要的佛塔是多层的楼阁式塔和密檐式塔等，塔形高大，如河北的料敌塔高达84米。

　　南传佛教地区的单层塔，有覆钵形塔，还有钟形塔，净瓶（方瓶）形塔及高棉式塔。虽是单层，但塔身很高，如缅甸仰光大金塔高达110多米。

　　藏传佛教地区的佛塔也是单层塔，俗称喇嘛塔。

泰国拍读清寿塔　　　　　日本法隆寺塔　　　　　泰国佛统大塔
（方瓶形塔）　　　　　　（楼阁式塔）　　　　　　（钟形塔）

　　佛塔主要结构有三部分，即塔基、塔身和塔刹。

　　佛塔的塔基是佛塔的基础，塔基又分基台和基座两部分。基台就是在地面上建造的规模较大的平台，一般较低矮。基座建在基台之上，而基座之上会兴建塔身。基座形制大小较为繁杂，常见的有须弥座和其他形制基座。一般是随塔身的形制，环境的特点而安排，有些基座还是佛塔雕塑艺术集中的区域。

　　塔身是佛塔的主要部分，塔身的结构形态决定了佛塔的形制。原始的佛塔的塔身是覆钵形的，后来出现了多种结构形态的塔身。

　　塔刹在佛塔的顶部，是佛塔一个极其重要的部分。所有佛塔都有塔刹，有塔必有刹。塔刹的重要意义和作用有以下三点：

　　一是宗教的意义。塔刹是佛国佛土的象征，是窣堵坡的象征，有的佛塔的塔刹就是一座小型的窣堵坡。

　　二是建筑结构的意义。佛塔修到顶，各构件要收拢一起，要封顶，要有一构件作收拢封盖，塔刹起到的就是这种作用。

　　三是建筑艺术的意义。很多塔刹的构造多种多样、多姿多彩。塔刹往往

| 泰国清迈佛塔塔刹 | 日本药师寺东塔塔刹 | 山西五台白塔塔刹 |

是全塔艺术处理的顶峰。

　　不论何种类型的佛塔，其塔刹的结构基本可分为三部分，即刹座、刹身和刹顶。

　　刹座。刹座下封盖塔身，上承托刹身。看一座佛塔，塔身和塔刹的分界线在哪里？就看塔身顶端封顶的那个构件，也就是塔身和塔刹的结合部位，这个构件就是塔刹的基座。

　　刹座的形式多样，如宝匣、覆钵、覆斗、圆形或多角素面柱。最常见的是宝匣，有的叫方箱、平头等。南亚和东南亚地区佛塔的塔刹，其刹座多数是宝匣，日本佛塔的刹座都是宝匣。喇嘛塔的刹座及中国佛塔的金属塔刹的刹座则是多角素面柱。

　　在宝匣或素面柱之上，往往添置多层仰莲或莲瓣，这些都是刹座的部分。

　　刹身。刹身基本是由相轮组成，相轮上部设宝盖（华盖）。相轮的形态结构和构成材质差别很大。南亚和东南亚佛塔的相轮多是由砖石等构件雕刻而成，喇嘛塔的相轮也是雕刻而成的，这些雕刻的相轮，其形状是圆锥形的。而各国佛塔的金属相轮则是环状构件串接而成，其形状有圆锥形的、也有直筒形、或纺锤形的。相轮的层数不一，一般在 3 至 13 层之间。

相轮上端有的设宝盖（华盖），宝盖往往成为刹身和刹顶的分界线，有的佛塔的宝盖下垂若干缆索系于塔身以固定塔刹。有些佛塔的宝盖还是艺术造型之处，喇嘛塔的宝盖极其华丽，其宝盖面积较大、构造复杂，宝盖周边下垂流苏、风铎等装饰品。为求稳固，宝盖下部设若干支撑固定于相轮周围。

刹顶。宝盖之上就是刹顶，刹顶的构造最为丰富多彩。砖石材质的塔刹，其刹顶较为简单，多数是宝珠，或双宝珠，或是葫芦状宝珠，泰国等地的塔刹，其刹顶则是宝伞。金属塔刹的刹顶花样较多，一般的刹顶有仰月、宝珠。有的刹顶还有圆光或水烟、宝瓶、宝盖、太阳、风向标等构件。

Pagodas appeared as Buddhism was created and developed. When Sakyamuni's body was cremated after his death, his disciples collected the relics and kept these relics and other remains of Sakyamuni inside the tomb-like construction, which was the early form of pagodas. Pagodas later spread to different parts of Asia as Buddhism was introduced to these areas.

Historically, Buddhism spread through three major routes. One was from ancient India to Sri Lanka, and to Burma, Thailand, Laos, Cambodia and Indonesia eastward, thus the name Southern Buddhism. Another route was from ancient India to Central Asia northward, and to China, Korean Peninsula, Japan, and Vietnam eastward, thus the name Han Buddhism. The third route was from ancient India to Tibet, China, and later to Chinese mainland and Mongolia, thus the name Tibetan Buddhism.

Pagodas were built in the places where Buddhism was introduced. Their forms vary greatly in different areas due to the differences in geographical characteristics and culture, such as single-storey pagodas in Southern Buddhism areas and Tibetan Buddhism areas, and multi-storey pagodas in Han Buddhism areas. Generally, the pagodas in Han Buddhism areas are multi-storey pavilion style and multi-eaved structures, most of which are large-sized, such as Liaodi

Pagoda in Hebei province, 84 meters in height.

Pagodas in Southern Buddhism areas are usually single-storey in the style of inverted-bowl, bell, square bottle and khmer. Single-storey as they are, the buildings are very tall, such as Rangoon Shwe Dagon Pagoda in Burma, with a height of more than 110 meters.

Pagodas in Tibetan Buddhism areas are also single-storey in structure, commonly known as Lamaist pagodas.

A Buddhist pagoda is composed of the three major parts: base, body and spire.

The base of pagodas consists of platform and pedestal. The platform is a large terrace built on the ground and is usually low. On top of the platform is the pedestal, and the body of pagodas is built right on the pedestal. The form and size of pedestals are quite diverse. Diamond Throne and pedestals of other forms are commonly seen, which are designed according to the form of main body and surrounding. Some pedestals become the most prominent part of the pagoda for the gorgeous sculpture on them.

The body of pagodas is the main part of the buildings, the form of which is determined by their structures. Originally, the pagoda body is in the style of inverted-bowl, but as time goes by, different styles of pagoda body have come into being.

Spire is an indispensable part for any Buddhist pagoda and every pagoda is surmounted by a spire. The significance and function of a spire are reflected in terms of religion, architectural structure and aesthetics. Spires are the symbol of stupa, representing land or territory of Buddha and the spire of some pagodas is a miniature of stupa itself. The spire is the tip of the building and the rafters, sheathing and tile ridges all come to one point, where a component should be fixed to stabilize the roof structure. The spire performs these functions. The structure of many spires is varied and graceful and the construction of them may display the peak of aesthetic treatment of the whole pagoda.

The spire is mainly composed of three parts: bottom, body and top.

The base of the spire is built on the roof of the pagoda with the spire body on its top. Spire bases vary from one another; most are shaped like square platform, blooming lotus petals, inverted bowl, inverted Dou, round or multiangular column. There is a heavenly palace in some pagodas, mostly inside the spire bases.

Discs, called Xianglun, form the main part of the spire body, above which an umbrellalike canopy is usually built. The types of discs differ, usually in the shape of cone, straight column, and spindle. For most discs, the ring–form components are fastened around the pole of the spire, while some other discs are carved on the conical components. The number of tiers varies, generally ranging from three to thirteen.

The structure of the spire top takes the most diversified forms, commonly consisting of components in the shape of crescent moon, precious bead, and precious umbrella. Components such as precious bottle, canopy, circular polarization, water smoke, the sun, blooming lotus petals, cucurbit, wind vane, and a giant precious bead can also be seen on top of the spire of some pagodas.

南传佛教
地区佛塔的特点

Features of Pagodas in Southern Buddhism Areas

　　南传佛教流行于南亚和东南亚地区。这个地区的佛塔基本都是单层塔。多数这种单层塔又高又大，如仰光大金塔高达 110 多米。这种塔不但塔身又高又尖，塔刹也又高又尖。一些佛塔把基座也修得又大又高。

　　南传佛教地区佛塔的形制，有覆钵形的，流行在斯里兰卡及印度与尼泊尔。有钟形的，多见于缅甸、泰国等地。还有一种方形塔，据说也是从古印度的某种建筑形式演化而来的，成为方瓶形佛塔，流行于老挝、泰国等地。如泰国读拍侬佛塔和老挝塔銮佛塔等。还有一种形似玉米棒形的圆形尖塔，即高棉式佛塔，多见于柬埔寨、泰国等地，如泰国郑王庙内的高棉式塔。

　　关于钟形佛塔，在覆钵形塔渐次增高过程中，钟形佛塔的塔身有几种不同的状况。泰国洛坤佛塔的塔身是一完整的钟形；佛统大塔的塔身一部分是光滑的钟形，一部分是有皱褶的圆锥形；仰光大金塔的塔身只有一小部分是光滑的钟形，大部分是有皱褶的圆锥形。无论哪种状况，整体看都是钟形塔。

　　在缅甸等东南亚国家，很多佛塔在主塔周围还建造很多小塔，其形制基本与主塔相似，形成大小组合的塔群。如仰光大金塔、金边塔銮及婆罗浮屠塔群等。

南传佛教地区佛塔，多数佛塔具有高大基座，形制不规则。

南传佛教地区佛塔的塔刹基本相似，刹座、刹身、刹顶齐全。刹座大多是宝匣（方箱），刹身多是雕刻的相轮，刹顶多数是金伞、少数是宝珠。

Southern Buddhism prevails in South Asia and Southeast Asia. Pagodas in these areas are mainley tall and huge single-storey pagodas. ShweDagon Pagoda is 110 meters tall. The tall and sharp body and spire of pagodas are usually built in order to make the pagodas look grand and some pagodas are also designed with a huge base.

There are different styles of pagodas in Southern Buddhism areas such as inverted bowl style commonly seen in Sri Lanka, India and Nepal, and bell-shaped style in Burma and Thailand, square-bottle-shaped style mainly in Laos and Thailand, which is said to be evolved from some kind of architecture in ancient India. Another type is corn-shaped round pagoda with a sharp spire, also called Khmer style pagoda mostly seen in Cambodia, Thailand and other Asian countries. In some Southeast Asian courtiers such as Burma, many pagodas include a main pagoda and some surrounding small pagodas, the forms of which are quite similar to that of the main building, forming a group of pagodas of different sizes.

The spire of the pagodas in Southern Buddhism areas has its own characteristics that base, body and top can all be found. The spire base is mostly shaped like square platform, and the body is Xianglun. The spire top is usually shaped like golden umbrella, and a few is precious bead. The spire and body of some pagodas, by contrast, are closely connected, which makes it hard to identify the limits of both parts. The pagodas in the areas are commonly built with a huge base of irregular forms.

汉传
佛教地区佛塔的特点
Features of Pagodas in Han Buddhism Areas

　　汉传佛教在中国兴盛发展，并进而影响到朝鲜半岛、日本及越南等地。中国的佛塔是按中国的文化传统发展起来的，主要是兴建多层的高塔，而将窣堵坡置于塔顶。这种高塔主要有楼阁式塔和密檐式塔，其他如金刚宝座塔及亭阁式塔等单层塔数目很少。

　　中国最早的佛塔是东汉时建造的楼阁式塔。楼阁式塔有多层（多至十三层），有层间结构，内有塔梯，可以登临。密檐式塔也是一种大型佛塔，第一层比例特大，第一层以上塔檐紧密相连，没有层间结构，一般不能登临，密檐式塔一般有高大基座，基座和塔的第一层布满艺术作品。

　　日本的佛塔多为木塔，基本属于楼阁式，虽然分层，但层间很短，出檐很大，不能登临。朝鲜半岛上的佛塔多为石塔，塔为实心，不能登临，有的像楼阁式，有的像密檐式。越南佛塔基本属于中国式的楼阁塔，有层间结构，可以登临。

　　汉传佛教佛塔的塔刹呈多样化。日本木塔的塔刹，其形制基本相同，刹座为方箱（宝匣），上为九层相轮，刹顶多为水烟和宝珠。朝鲜半岛石塔的塔刹多数是石质塔刹，有的已残损。朝鲜半岛石塔少数是金属塔刹，结构完整。其刹座多为方箱或多角素面柱，上有相轮，有的设宝盖，刹顶多为水烟和宝珠。

中国佛塔的塔刹较为繁杂。较早的砖石塔，其塔刹是砖石雕刻出来的，这些砖石塔刹结构简单，其中有少数尚完好，如嵩岳寺塔、大雁塔及玄奘墓塔等，有不少已残损，如登封法王寺塔、虎丘塔及延安宝塔等。

宋辽以后建造的佛塔，其塔刹往往是金属的，但这些金属塔刹，其造型五花八门。一些金属塔刹结构完整、内容丰富，如雷峰塔、应县木塔及通州燃灯塔等。它们都有刹座、相轮，刹顶都有仰月、水烟和宝珠等。有一些金属塔刹则很简陋，一个显著特点是没有相轮，如定州料敌塔。有几座佛塔的塔刹十分特殊，如开封铁塔的塔刹，只是在圆形座上接了一个圆球；又如颐和园琉璃塔的塔刹，宝盖上只接一只法铃（铃铛）。

Han Buddhism thrives and evolves in China and exerts some influence on Korean Peninsula, Japan and Vietnam. Pagodas in China have been designed and constructed on the basis of Chinese traditions and culture, and a large number of multi-storey high pagodas have been erected with a stupa on their top. This kind of high pagodas is mainly in the style of pavilion and multi-eaved, whereas single-storey pagodas like vajrasana pagodas and single-storey pavilion-style pagodas are quite few.

The first pagoda in China was built in East Han dynasty and in the style of pavilion. The buildings are usually multi-storey, 13 storeys at the most, with stairs inside for people to step up to the pagoda top. Another type of large-sized pagoda is multi-eaved structures with a huge base. The first storey of such building is large in height, while the upper storeys are closely attached to each other, which makes it impossible for people to climb up. The huge base and the first storey of the buildings are densely decorated with the works of art.

Pagodas in Japan are mostly made out of wood and in pavilion-style. While there are storeys inside, the short height of the storeys and long overhang eaves make it impossible for people to climb up the pagodas. Most pagodas in Korean Peninsula, shaped as a pavilion or multi-eaved, are made of stone and solid inside, and thus there is no access for climbers. Pagodas in Vietnam, basically belonging to Chinese-style pavilion structure, are built with storeys and stairs inside that enable climbers to go up to the top.

Spires of the pagodas in Han Buddhism areas are diversified. Those of wooden pagodas in Japan are similar in their forms, which consist of a base shaped as square platform, nine-layer discs, and a spire top shaped as water smoke and precious bead. The spires of stone pagodas in Korean Peninsula look like those in Japan, most of which are composed of a base shaped as square platform or multiangular column, discs, some decorated with a canopy, and a top shaped as water smoke and precious bead.

Spires of the pagodas in China take the most diverse forms. The spires of the early brick and stone pagodas are carved out of bricks and stones, which are simple in structure. Few of the such spires are in good condition, such as Songyue Temple Pagoda, Big Wild Goose Pagoda and Xuanzang Tomb Pagoda. Some other spires have been damaged, such as Fawang Temple Pagoda, Tiger Hill Pagoda and Yan'an Pagoda.

Spires of the Pagodas built after Song and Liao dynasties are mainly made of metal, and vary in their forms. Some of the metal spires are complete in structure, consisting of a base, discs, and a top with crescent moon, water smoke and precious bead, such as Leifeng Pagoda, Yingxian Wooden Pagoda and Randeng Pagoda.

By contrast, the spires of some other pagodas, such as Liaodi Pagoda in Dingzhou city, have a quite simple structure, some of which are built even without discs. A few pagodas have a spire different from other spires. The Kaifeng Iron Pagoda has a spire with only a round base toped with a round ball.

藏传佛教
地区佛塔的特点

Features of Pagodas in Tibetan Buddhism Areas

　　藏传佛教主要流传在中国和蒙古国。藏传佛教的佛塔受到尼泊尔和藏族文化的影响，俗称喇嘛塔。喇嘛塔也是单层塔，其塔身多变化，有的塔身就是一块圆石头，常见的喇嘛塔塔身是一倒瓶形体，上端稍大，或有削肩。有的喇嘛塔塔身辟焰光门，供奉佛像或其他佛教圣物。

　　喇嘛塔一般有较大基座，基座基本是多层多折角的须弥座。喇嘛塔的基座也有其他形式，有的就是一座收分很大的藏式塔楼。

　　喇嘛塔塔刹可谓豪华。塔刹刹座是多边折角须弥座或多角素面柱，刹身是一硕大雕塑的相轮，其上是绚丽多彩的宝盖。刹顶多数是由一座小型喇嘛塔的塔身和多连葫芦状宝珠组成。北海白塔的刹顶是由仰月、太阳和火焰宝珠组成。

　　Tibetan Buddhism mainly prevails in China and Mongolia. Pagodas in Tibetan Buddhism areas are largely influenced by the culture of Nepal and Tibetan culture, commonly known as Lamaist pagodas. Lamaist pagodas are single-storey and the form of the main body is diverse. The body of some pagodas is a round

rock, or a single-storey folk building.

Lamaist pagodas usually have a large pedestal, generally a multi-layered, multi-angular Diamond Throne, which is a bit larger, sometimes with sloping shoulders. There are other types of pedestals, some of which are Tibetan building.

The spires of Lamaist pagodas may be described as "splendid". The spire body is a huge Xianglun, with a gorgeous canopy on its top. The base of most spires is Diamond Throne. The spire top is usually a small Lamaist pagoda, or cucurbit-shaped precious beads. Some Lamaist pagodas have a spire top composed of crescent moon, the sun, and precious beads.

南传佛教
地区的佛塔

Pagodas in Southern Buddhism Areas

尼泊尔斯瓦杨布佛塔

Swayambhunath Nepal

斯瓦杨布佛塔邮票（*尼泊尔 2006 年发行*）

　　斯瓦杨布佛塔位于尼泊尔加德满都市郊西北小山顶上，是一覆钵式塔，塔身白色，塔身高约 10 米，塔基直径 20 米。该佛塔是斯瓦杨布寺内的主体建筑。

　　佛塔建筑年代说法不一，有说建于 3 世纪、有说 4 世纪，也有说建于公元前的，总的来说，佛塔已有近两千年的历史了，传说佛祖曾驾临此地。斯瓦杨布佛塔已被列入世界文化遗产。

　　斯瓦杨布佛塔的塔刹极为壮观。塔刹底部为一方形体，即为宝匣。宝匣

之上是十三层镀金相轮，相轮之上是宝盖，宝盖之上是高数米的由数枚宝珠组成的镀金宝顶。整个塔刹金光闪闪，阳光下熠熠生辉。宝盖周边悬挂数十铜铃，微风过处，铃声飘扬。

斯瓦杨布佛塔的精彩之处也是在塔刹之处，即塔刹底部的宝匣。宝匣四面各有一双大眼睛，那是智慧之眼，亦是佛眼。不论你处于佛塔的哪个方向，佛眼都会看着你。

在尼泊尔有不少佛塔，其塔刹宝匣的四周也都有眼睛。

斯瓦杨布佛塔（邑石网供图）

Located on the top of a hill in the Kathmandu Valley, west of Kathmandu city, Nepal, the pagoda, with its white body, is in the inverted-bowl style. It is the main building of Swayambhunath temple, which is about 10 meters high and has a base 20 meters in diameter.

There are different versions as to the date of its construction. Some people insist that the pagoda was built in the 3rd or 4th century, while some others believe that the building may date back to B.C. In any case, the pagoda has a history of more than 2000 years. It is said that the site used to be visited by Buddha. Now it has been listed as World Heritage Site.

The spire of the pagoda looks magnificent, which consists of a cubical base topped with gilded discs of thirteen tiers and a canopy. The gilded top of the spire is comprised of some precious beads, totally several meters in height. The whole spire is sparkling in the sunlight and there are dozens of bells hanging around the canopy, ringing in the breeze.

Another striking feature of the pagoda is that the cubical structure of the spire base is painted with eyes of Buddha looking in all four directions, which represent wisdom and compassion. Many other pagodas in Nepal also have eyes on each of the four sides of the spire.

斯里兰卡阿巴耶祇利佛塔

Abhayagiri Pagoda Sri Lanka

（斯里兰卡 1997 年发行）
阿巴耶祇利佛塔邮票

（斯里兰卡 1980 年发行）
阿巴耶祇利佛塔邮票

　　阿巴耶祇利佛塔，也称无畏山寺塔，位于斯里兰卡阿努拉达普拉古城，建于公元前 89 年，现塔高 75 米，是覆钵式佛塔。

　　此塔建成后，继续维修扩建，到公元 2 世纪佛塔增高至 100 米，据中国高僧法显描述，此塔原高 122 米并饰以金银。

　　无畏山寺是斯里兰卡著名古寺，公元 410 年，我国东晋时期高僧法显曾到此修行两年，回国时带回数部重要佛经。

　　塔刹的底部是宝匣，其上是圆锥形刹体，许是相轮。由于年代久远，刹体顶端已损坏，毁去约五分之一，刹顶也就不见了。

　　Located in the Sacred City of Anuradhapura，Sri Lanka，Abhayagiri Pagoda was constructed in 89 B.C. The extant building is an inverted-bowl structure，75 meters in height.

　　Following the restoration and extension in the 2nd century A.D.， the pagoda used to stand over 100 meters tall. Based on the accounts of Faxian，a Chinese Buddhist monk，the pagoda was originally made of red bricks，with a height of 122 meters，and decorated with gold and silver. Allegedly， the construction took 27 years， and 73.3 million baked bricks were used.

Abhayagiri is one of the famous monasteries in Sri Lanka. Faxian， a Chinese Buddhist monk in East Jin dynasty， used to lead his monastic life here for two years and brought some important Buddhist Scriptures back to China.

The base of the spire is in the shape of square platform， topped with a conical spire body. The upper part of the spire has been damaged as time goes by， and as a result， the spire top no longer exists.

阿巴耶祇利佛塔 （邑石网供图）

斯里兰卡祇陀梵那（祇陀林）佛塔

Jetavanaramaya Sri Lanka

（斯里兰卡1997年发行）
祇陀梵那佛塔邮票

（斯里兰卡1980年发行）
祇陀梵那佛塔邮票

　　祇陀梵那佛塔，也称祇陀林佛塔。位于斯里兰卡阿努拉达普拉古城。建于公元 4 世纪，祇陀梵那佛塔是由一位国王始建，由其子（公元 303—331 年在位）续建完成。现塔高 70 米，塔基直径约 112 米，是一座典型的覆钵式佛塔。据说塔内藏有佛祖用过的束腰带。佛塔建在巨大的台基之上，佛塔用砖砌成，其外涂以白色。因时间久远，雪白的外壳脱落，只留下了黯淡的砖色。

　　塔刹底部是硕大的宝匣（方箱），宝匣之上就是圆锥形刹体，许是相轮，刹体已毁去一半，刹顶已经不见。

　　Jetavanaramaya is located in the Sacred City of Anuradhapura, Sri Lanka. A historical king of Sri Lanka initiated the construction of the pagoda in the 4th century A.D., and his son (303—331) completed the construction. The extant pagoda is an inverted-bowl structure, 70 meters in height, with a base 112

南传佛教地区的佛塔

meters in diameter. A part of a sash or belt tied by the Buddha is believed to be the relic that is enshrined here.

Built on a huge platform，the pagoda was constructed of red bricks. The building was originally coated with white paint which has disappeared after many years' erosion. What can be seen today is the dark bricks.

The base of the spire is in the shape of square platform，topped with a conical spire body. The upper part of the spire has been damaged，and as a result，the spire top no longer exists.

祇陀梵那佛塔（邑石网供图）

斯里兰卡鲁梵维利萨亚佛塔
Ruwanwelisaya Pagoda Sri Lanka

（斯里兰卡 1947 年发行）
鲁梵维利萨亚佛塔邮票

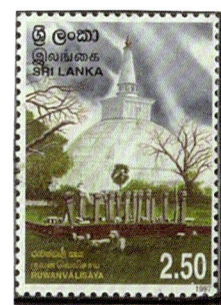

（斯里兰卡 1997 年发行）
鲁梵维利萨亚佛塔邮票

  鲁梵维利萨亚佛塔，位于阿努拉达普拉古城，佛塔始建于公元前 2 世纪。传塔内藏佛骨舍利，塔内还发现公元 2 世纪的象牙雕像和佛珠等珍贵文物。

  鲁梵维利萨亚佛塔现高 100 米，塔基直径 96 米。这是一座白色覆钵式塔。塔的规模为全岛最大，故也称"大塔"。

  佛塔塔身上部是塔刹，塔刹底部是方箱（宝匣），其上为一圆锥形石柱，刻有相轮，相轮较密。刹顶为葫芦宝珠，表面镀金。

  佛塔的围墙外侧，排满大象雕塑，极为壮观。

  Located in the Sacred City of Anuradhapura, Sri Lanka, the pagoda was constructed in the 2nd century B.C. It is believed that Buddhist relics are enshrined in the pagoda, and other valuable cultural relics such as ivory statues and Buddhist prayer beads, which date back to the 2nd century, have been found inside the building.

The Ruwanwelisaya is a hemispherical structure，100 meters tall，with a base 96 meters in diameter. The white inverted-bowl style pagoda is the largest monument in the country，thus also known as "Big Pagoda".

The base of the spire is in the shape of square platform，topped with a conical spire body carved with discs of dense tiers. On top of the spire is a cucurbit-like precious bead with gilding.

Outside of the walls are lined with statues of elephants，which make the site magnificent.

鲁梵维利萨亚佛塔(邑石网供图)

斯里兰卡图帕拉玛佛塔

Thuparama Pagoda Sri Lanka

图帕拉玛佛塔邮票（斯里兰卡 1997 年发行）

　　图帕拉玛佛塔，位于斯里兰卡波隆纳鲁沃古城，是一座覆钵式佛塔。是此地最大佛塔，是斯里兰卡第四高塔。塔内供奉佛祖的锁骨和一钵的佛碎身舍利子。

　　图帕拉玛佛塔始建于公元前 250—前 210 年，佛塔之下有数排花岗岩石柱，以前曾有高大建筑物罩在佛塔之上。

　　图帕拉玛佛塔塔刹下为宝匣，上为相轮，相轮密度较稀，刹顶为葫芦状双宝珠。

　　Located in the sacred area of Anuradhapura, Sri Lanka, Thuparama Pagoda is the largest and the fourth tallest monument built in the island. The pagoda is an inverted-bowl style structure, in which the collarbone of the Buddha and other Buddhist relics are enshrined.

　　The Thuparama Pagoda was first built in the years of 250B.C.—210 B.C. The

compound, used to be covered by another tall building, is paved with granite and surrounded by two rows of stone pillars.

The spire of the pagoda is comprised of three parts: a base shaped like square platform, discs with sparse tiers, and a top consisting of two precious beads in the shape of a cucurbit.

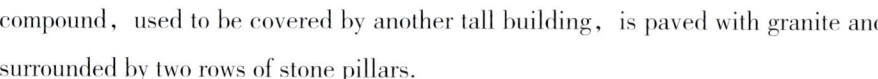

图帕拉玛佛塔（邑石网供图）

邮票上的

佛塔

Buddhist Pagodas Featured On Postage Stamps

斯里兰卡吉里昆诃罗佛塔
Kili Vehera Pagoda Sri Lanka

吉里昆诃罗佛塔邮票（斯里兰卡 1958 年发行）

吉里昆诃罗佛塔，位于斯里兰卡波隆纳鲁沃古城。塔高 80 英尺（约 24.5 米），是一座覆钵式佛塔。

吉里昆诃罗佛塔是在波罗迦罗摩巴忽大帝执政时期（公元 1153—1186 年）修建的。

吉里昆诃罗塔刹底部是宝匣，其上是密密的圆锥柱相轮。刹顶是一金色的圆锥，相轮和刹顶连在一起，是一个完整的圆锥体。

Located in the ancient City of Polonnaruwa, Sri Lanka, Kili Vehera Pagoda is an inverted-bowl style structure, 24.5 meters tall. It was constructed during the reign of Parakramabahu I (1153–1186).

The pagoda has a base in the shape of square platform, above which there are discs of dense tiers and a golden spire top. The discs and the top form a shape of an integrated cone.

南传佛教地区的佛塔

吉里昆诃罗佛塔（邑石网供图）

印度摩诃菩提金刚宝座塔

Maha Bodhi Pagoda India

印度摩诃菩提金刚宝座塔邮票（中国 2008 年发行）

印度摩诃菩提金刚宝座塔位于印度比哈尔邦城南的菩提迦耶。此处是释迦牟尼悟道处，古代遗迹包括菩提树、摩诃菩提寺等。古代遗迹在公元 1861 年被发现，公元 1870 年修复。

摩诃菩提寺也称为大菩提寺，摩诃菩提寺的主体是一座金刚宝座塔，主塔呈方形，高 50 米。塔体由下而上逐渐收缩，成为方锥柱形。塔体用硬质砂岩建造，主塔四角各建一小塔，塔形似主塔，主塔内供奉佛祖金身像一座。

金刚宝座塔主塔和小塔的顶部是塔刹。塔刹实际是一座小型覆钵式塔，此小塔上部又是一组塔刹。其刹座为宝匣，上为相轮、宝盖和宝珠。

Maha Bodhi pagoda is located in Bodh Gaya, Bihar state, India, where the Buddha is said to have attained enlightenment. The site, containing a Bodhi Tree and the Mahabodhi Temple, was discovered in 1861 and restored in 1870.

The pagoda is the main building of Mahabodhi Temple，the central part of which is square in shape and 50 meters in height. The structure decreases in size as it rises，forming a shape of a pyramid. The pagoda is constructed of calley-stone, surrounded by four smaller pagodas in same style. A golden statue of Buddha is enshrined inside the main building.

The central pagoda and the four smaller ones include a spire on their tops, which is virtually a small-sized pagoda of inverted-bowl style. On top of it is another spire with a base shaped like square platform，topped with discs，canopy and a precious bead.

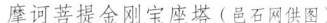

摩诃菩提金刚宝座塔（邑石网供图）

缅甸仰光大金塔

Rangoon ShweDagon Pagoda Burma

仰光大金塔邮票（缅甸 1956 年发行）

仰光大金塔位于仰光北郊茵雅湖畔圣山上，塔高 112 米，是典型的钟形佛塔。

始建年代说法不 ， 说建丁公元前 585 年，又说有文献记载，是在佛祖逝世前，该塔已建。但据考古学者认为该塔是在 6—10 世纪建造。后几经扩建，直到 15 世纪才修到 98 米。现塔是在公元 1774 年由贡榜王朝辛漂信王修建的。

传说，早年当地有两名商人运一船大米去印度救灾，回来时带回八根佛祖头发，国王因此建此塔供奉此佛舍利。

仰光大金塔是建在一块大理石铺的地面上。地面上是大金塔的塔基，塔基是八角十字折角形的须弥座。塔基上周围建 54 座小塔和 4 座中型塔。塔基中央建主塔，主塔现高 112 米，塔基面积为 115 平方米。

仰光大金塔塔身全部敷金，整个佛塔金光闪耀，大小塔身贴有 1000 多张金箔。塔内供奉一尊玉佛像。

塔刹结构豪华，塔刹底层是仰莲须弥座，莲座之上是宝瓶、相轮、宝伞，其上是金属相轮，再上是风向标，顶端是大宝珠。金伞周围悬金铃和银铃。金伞中有金球，球上镶红宝石、翡翠和钻石。刹顶是一颗大钻石。

The ShweDagon Pagoda is located on Singuttara Hill, in the city of Rangoon, Burma. It is a typical bell-shaped structure, standing 112 meters in height.

There is no agreement as to the date of its construction. A legend goes that the pagoda was constructed in 585 B.C. before Buddha passed away. According to tradition, two merchant brothers sent relief to India where a disaster broke out, and they brought back eight of the Buddha's hairs when they returned to Burma. The king commissioned the construction of the pagoda in honor of this great event.

仰光大金塔夜景（邑石网供图）

However, archaeologists believe that the pagoda was built between the 6th and 10th centuries A.D. Some renovations were made later, and as a result the pagoda was raised to its current height of 98 meters till the 15th century. The extant structure was constructed by the King Hsinbyushin.

The pagoda was erected on the ground paved with marbles. The base covers an area of 115 square meters, above which there are terraces in the shape of octagonal Sumeru pedestal. The main building is surrounded by 54 small pagodas and 4 middle-sized pagodas.

Built on the central part of the base, the main body of the pagoda, 112 meters tall, in which a jade statue of Buddha is enshrined, is covered with gold plates. It is said that more than a thousand gold plates are used for the pagodas.

The spire of the pagoda has luxurious components. At the bottom is the blooming lotus petals, topped with precious bottle, discs and canopy. Atop the canopy are metal discs, wind vane, and a big precious bead. Gold and silver bells hang around the umbrella-like canopy which is decorated with gold balls inlaid with rubies, jade and diamond. A big diamond is fixed to the very top of the spire.

泰国玉佛寺三塔

Jade Buddha Temple Three Pagodas Thailand

（日本 1987 年发行）

玉佛寺三塔邮票

（泰国 1970 年发行）

玉佛寺三塔邮票

　　三塔位于泰国大王宫玉佛寺，建于公元 1784 年。在玉佛寺大雄宝殿北面有一大台基，台基上有三座宏大的建筑，从西向东排成一行。西端第一座为舍利塔，第二座是藏经楼，第三座是万神殿。

　　舍利塔高 40 米，是钟形塔。塔内供奉佛祖胸骨舍利。舍利塔塔刹是由方箱、相轮、圆锥状刹顶组成，顶端是宝珠。

　　藏经楼是泰式风格，方形尖顶，围以柱廊。有介绍说，内部有藏经橱，其内供奉一部由国王拉玛一世写的以金片制的佛经。

　　万神殿是高棉式，内有拉玛一世至五世泰国国王纪念像。万神殿是玉佛寺最高建筑。

Located in Jade Buddha Temple, also known as Temple of the Emerald Buddha, Thailand, the pagodas were constructed in 1784. Built on the huge terrace to the immediate north of Chapel, the main hall of the temple, the three

grand buildings are lined from west to east, including the pagoda of relics known as Phra Sri Rattana Chedi on the west, the library known as the Phra Mondop in the middle, and Pantheon known as Dhosa Kiridhorn.

Phra Sri Rattana Chedi is a bell-shaped structure, 40 meters tall, housing a piece of the Buddha's breastbone. The spire of the pagoda is comprised of square platform, discs and a conical top with a precious bead at its very top.

The library is in Thai style, square in shape, with a spire on the top, and surrounded by columns. The library houses bookcases in which the Tripitaka (sacred Buddhist manuscripts) written by the king Rama I were preserved.

The Pantheon, the tallest building in the Temple of the Emerald Buddha, is in Cambodian style, where one can see the portraits of the kings from Rama I to Rama V.

从西向东排列的三塔(邑石网供图)

泰国读拍侬佛塔

Phanom Pagoda Thailand

读拍侬佛塔邮票（泰国 1971 年发行）

　　读拍侬佛塔位于泰国那空拍侬府达拍侬县，与老挝甘蒙省隔河相望。是一座净瓶（方瓶）形佛塔，塔高 57.5 米。

　　相传两千年前，佛祖曾飞到此地，并许愿身后将部分骨灰赠予此地。佛祖圆寂后，其弟子摩诃迦叶护送佛陀胸骨舍利至此并建塔供奉，在当地五位国王的协助下，建成此塔。11 世纪时，老挝国王曾亲自来此礼拜。

　　读拍侬佛塔相传始建年代约在 7—8 世纪，也有的说是 5 世纪，也有的说是 10 世纪的。根据塔的艺术形制，应在 9 世纪前后建成。

　　读拍侬佛塔原属老挝，公元 1886 年法国殖民者和暹罗划分领土后，将此塔划归泰国。泰国政府还在公元 1940 年维修此塔，并再次增高塔身。

　　公元 1975 年因雨塌毁，泰国政府再建，公元 1979 年完工，即现塔。

　　公元 1979 年维修佛塔时，发现塔内藏有铜盒，铜盒里外共六层，最里层确实藏有佛陀舍利。读拍侬佛塔有四门，但都不能开启，塔身刻有羽翎卷草纹和藤蔓卷草纹，镶有武士、狮子等雕塑。

　　塔刹高 4.5 米，由刹座、相轮、仰月和金伞组成，金伞敷金。

Phra That Phanom Chedi is located in Nakhon Phanom province, Thailand, just across the river from Khammouane province of Laos. It is a Buddhist pagoda in the shape of square bottle, 57.5 meters tall.

Legend has it that 2000 years ago, the Buddha flew to this place and promised to give away some of his ashes. After the Buddha's death, his disciple Mahakasyapa escorted the Buddha's breast bone to this place, and with the help of five local Kings, he built a pagoda at the site to enshrine the relics. In the 11th century, the king of Laos himself came to the place to worship.

The pagoda is thought to have been built sometime in the 7th to 8th centuries, but judged from the style of the structure, it must have been constructed around the 9th century. The pagoda was originally a part of Laos, but after the French colonists and Siamese divided the territory in 1886, it has been put under the administration of Thailand. The Thailand government rebuilt the

读拍侬佛塔（邑石网供图）

building in 1940 and raised it to its current height. Because of the heavy rains in 1975, the pagoda was badly damaged and was renovated again by the government. The renovation work was completed in 1979.

A six-tiered bronze box was discovered inside the pagoda during the renovation work in 1979, where the relics of Buddha was enshrined. There are four doors in the pagoda which are rarely open. The outside walls of the building are decorated with designs of grass, and inlaid with statues of warriors and lions.

The spire of the pagoda, 4.5 meters in height, is comprised of a base, discs and other components in the shape of crescent moon and precious umbrella coated with gold.

泰国佛统金塔
Pathom Chedi Thailand

佛统金塔邮票（泰国1971年发行）

　　佛统金塔又名帕巴吞佛塔，位于泰国佛统府佛统市中心。是一座钟形佛塔。塔高120米，塔基直径50多米。

　　该塔据说始建于7世纪，只有39米。公元1853年拉玛四世国王重建新塔，拉玛五世又扩建，才成今塔。这三个不同时期建的塔，不是对老塔推倒重建，而是在老塔外套建新塔。

　　佛塔的圆形塔基有两层。塔刹部分高40米，塔刹底是宝匣，上为相轮，刹顶为宝伞。

　　金塔中有一尊金佛，一尊卧佛，以及珍贵的佛骨舍利。

　　Phra Pathommachedi, also known as Phra Pathom Chedi, is located in the town center of Nakhon Pathom, Nakhon Pathom province, Thailand. The bell-shaped building is 120 meters tall and has a base with a diameter of over 50 meters.

　　The pagoda was allegedly constructed in the 7th century, with a height of only

39 meters. It was rebuilt by the king Mongkut in 1853, and expanded later by the king Chulalongkorn. The original buildings were not replaced by the new ones, but were reconstructed just outside the previous structures. Therefore, the pagodas constructed in different stages are virtually one inside the other.

The pagoda has a round base of two layers. The spire of the building, 40 meters in height, is comprised of a bottom part shaped as square platform, discs and a spire top in the shape of precious umbrella.

Inside the pagoda there are a golden statue of Buddha, a statue of reclining Buddha and some valuable relics of Buddha.

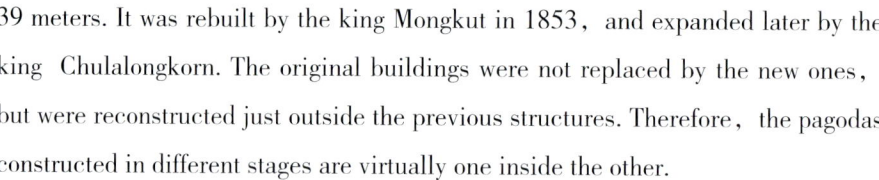

佛统金塔（邑石网供图）

佛统大金塔夜景（邑石网供图）

泰国洛坤佛塔

Muang Nakhom Pagoda Thailand

洛坤佛塔邮票（泰国1973年发行）

　　洛坤佛塔位于泰国洛坤府玛哈泰寺内，人称洛坤金塔。建于13—14世纪。塔高55.78米，佛塔是钟形塔。

　　洛坤金塔基座是正方梯形高台，基座周边建一圈小塔。台上中央是覆钟形塔身，塔身原涂白色。经多年风雨，变成黑灰色。

　　塔刹底层是宝匣（方箱），其四周有图案。宝匣之上是圆锥柱相轮，相轮很密，足有三四十层。刹顶是一细长的圆锥体，圆锥体全部敷金。顶端不是金伞，而是一颗宝珠。

　　Muang Nakhom Pagoda，also known as Great Noble Relics Stupa，is located in Wat Phra Mahathat Woramahawihan，the main Buddhist temple of Nakhon Si Thammarat province in southern Thailand. The bell-shaped building was constructed between the 13th and 14th centuries with a total height of 55.78 meters.

　　The base of the pagoda is high and in the square and trapezoidal shape， surrounded by a group of minor pagodas. At the center on the base is the main body of the structure painted in white. However, the color turns to dark grey after many years of erosion by wind and rain.

The spire of the pagoda is comprised of the bottom part in the shape of square platform, decorated with designs on its four sides, densely tiered conical discs, and the cone-shaped spire top coated with gold. A precious bead, instead of gold umbrella, is fixed to the very top of the spire.

洛坤金塔（邑石网供图）

泰国清迈佛塔

Chiengmai Wat Suan Dok Pagoda Thailand

清迈佛塔邮票（泰国 1971 年发行）

　　清迈佛塔位于泰国清迈府松德寺内。是一座巨大的钟形佛塔。

　　据传是为纪念锡兰著名僧人玛哈泰拉苏玛那而建。他来泰国讲学时曾住在此地。佛塔建在一巨大方形台座上，其上建多层圆形须弥座，座上建覆钟形塔身。

　　清迈佛塔塔刹结构简洁。塔刹下部是宝匣，宝匣四周为彩色图案，宝匣之上为圆锥形相轮，其上为长长的刹杆，刹杆上装多层宝伞。

Located in the Wat Suan Dok Temple in Chiengmai, northern Thailand, the pagoda is a huge bell-shaped structure. Legends tell that it was constructed to commemorate Sumana Thera, a famous monk of Ceylon who used to live in this area when he traveled to Thailand to give lectures. Built on a huge square platform, the inverted-bell style pagoda has a round and multi-layered Sumeru pedestal.

The spire of the pagoda is comparatively simple in structure, which is comprised of a spire base in the shape of square platform decorated with colored designs on its four sides, conical discs and a spire top shaped as multi-tiered precious umbrella fastened to a long pole.

清迈佛塔（邑石网供图）

泰国黎素贴佛塔

Doi Suthep Pagoda Thailand

黎素贴佛塔邮票（泰国1971年发行）

黎素贴塔位于泰国清迈府黎素贴山之巅，佛塔建于公元 1373 年。

当初兰纳王国的圭纳王（公元 1355—1385 年在位）邀请素可泰王国的高僧素玛那泰拉前往清迈讲学，他途中在邦加城获得一份佛舍利，圭纳王命人在该处建 5 米高的黎素贴佛塔，以供奉此舍利。公元 1538 年，兰纳国王重修佛塔，就是现塔。

塔身之上是塔刹，塔刹由刹座、相轮和金伞组成。

Located on the top of Doi Suthep, a mountain in Chiengmai province, Thailand, the pagoda is presumably constructed in 1373.

According to a legend, a monk named Sumanathera was invited to Chiengmai by King Nu Naone of Lan Na to give lectures and on his way he found a relic of Buddha. King Nu Naone ordered to build a five-meter-tall pagoda at the site to enshrine the relic Sumanathera took to them. The building was renovated by another king of Lan Na in 1538，which is the structure that we can see today.

The spire of the pagoda consists of a base，discs and an umbrella-shaped golden spire top.

黎素贴佛塔（邑石网供图）

泰国合里纹猜佛塔

That Hariphun Chai Pagoda Thailand

合里纹猜佛塔邮票（泰国1978年发行）

　　合里纹猜佛塔位于泰国南奔府直辖县。传说佛陀曾来过哈里奔猜山，并预言此地有金瓶供奉佛陀的额骨及指骨的舍利，以及一钵之多的碎身舍利。

　　公元877年，此城的阿提拉王将舍利从原藏处取出，并建造黄金佛塔以供奉舍利。

　　合里纹猜佛塔，在500多年前的提洛卡王时期，又一次重修，就是现塔。

　　佛塔是在方形塔基上，先建方形十字折角须弥座，在须弥座上是覆钵体塔身，覆钵体塔身之上是三层大小不同的平座，平座之上就是塔刹。

　　塔刹本身就是一座完整的覆钵式佛塔。塔刹底部就是覆钵式刹座，其上是圆锥形多层相轮，再上是金色宝伞。

　　That Hariphunchai Pagoda is located inside Wat Phrathat Hariphunchai at Lamphun，Thailand. Legend has it that the Buddha used to visit the mountain and predicted that there would be a gold bottle for the Buddha's crown of a skull, finger bones, phalanges, and a great number of other relics.

In 877, the king of Lamphun city, Athittayarat, took the relics out and ordered the construction of a golden pagoda to house the relics of the Buddha. The building was reconstructed as it stands today during the reign of King Tilokkarat about 500 years ago.

The pagoda has a square base, on which there are the square Sumeru pedestal, the inverted-bowl style main body, and the spire sitting on a three-layered platform.

The spire is in the shape of a complete inverted-bowl style pagoda, consisting of the base shaped as inverted-bowl, multi-tiered conical discs and the golden top shaped as precious umbrella.

合里纹猜佛塔(邑石网供图)

南传佛教地区的佛塔

泰国拍读清寿佛塔

That Choeng Chum Pagoda Thailand

拍读清寿佛塔邮票（泰国 1978 年发行）

　　拍读清寿佛塔位于泰国色军府直辖县。塔高 24 米，方形。塔内有佛祖留下的足印。每逢泰历 2 月 9 日至 15 日举行佛礼盛会。

　　拍读清寿佛塔建在寺庙中，地坪上为方形台，分五层逐渐收缩。台上建方形塔座，其上建方瓶形塔身。台基围以低矮栏杆，台基面辟门，以便出入。

　　塔刹很有特点，底层是宝匣，上为宝瓶，顶上有九层金伞，其上是四颗串在一起的宝珠。

Located in the center of Sakhon Nakhon town, Thailand, That Choeng Chum is 24 meters tall and of rectangular shape. Inside the building, the footprints of the Buddha are preserved. Grand Buddhist ceremony is held each year on the 9th to 15th, February.

The pagoda, mounted on a square base in the temple named Wat Phra That

Choeng Chum, has five tiers decreasing in size as they progress upward. The pagoda body shaped as square bottle sits on the square pedestal. The broad base is surrounded by low balustrades and has a door at the front side for access.

The spire of the pagoda is quite different from those of other pagodas in Thailand, which consists of a square platform, precious-bottle shaped body and nine-tiered golden umbrella topped by four precious beads.

拍读清寿佛塔(邑石网供图)

老挝万象塔銮佛塔

That Luang Pagoda Laos

（老挝 1990 年发行）万象塔銮邮票

（老挝 2000 年发行）万象塔銮邮票

　　塔銮，即皇家大塔，位于万象市以北约 5 公里处，是一净瓶（方瓶）式佛塔，主塔通高 45 米。

　　塔銮建于公元 737 年。但有的说建于 3 世纪，有的说是 6 世纪，还有说是 2000 多年前由阿育王所建。

　　初建时为一小塔，建在一个方形石墩上。公元 1566 年澜沧王塞塔提拉在小塔上建大塔。此后塔銮在 18 世纪遭多次破坏，现塔是公元 1930 年重建的，是由灰砖建造的。塔下埋有佛祖的骨舍利。

　　塔銮主塔塔高 45 米。主塔底部是一圆角锥形体基座，基座上主塔周围用 24 瓣大型莲花瓣围衬，上部是一方瓶形塔身。

　　塔銮塔基分两层。第一层塔基为方形，东西长 61.3 米，南北宽 58.48 米。塔基上建一圈堞叶，四个角各建一小塔，四周中间各建一座膜拜亭。膜拜亭有门，下通外廊的塔门，上通二层塔基的拱形门，中间有踏步相连。

　　第二层塔基也是正方形，每边长 48 米。第二层塔基分三层。外层由多个雕形莲瓣组成，中层由若干堞叶组成，堞叶中各有一尊佛像。里层是为纪念佛祖 30 种恩泽而建的 30 座小塔。小塔高 3.6 米，小塔内还设置一小金塔。

塔銮主塔塔身敷以金箔，整个佛塔金光闪闪，光耀夺目。

塔身之上是塔刹。塔刹十分繁复而有个性。底部是覆斗状刹座，上面是两层方箱，再上是方形莲座，其上是斗状方箱，再上是圆形莲座和宝瓶。其上是双层宝盖和一宝瓶，再上是两组宝盖和宝瓶相串接。刹顶是宝珠。

佛塔之外建一圈方形外廊，每边长 91 米。这些外廊除了存放一些祭祀用品外，主要是给僧侣们提供生活起居之用。

Pha That Luang，also known as Great Stupa，is located five kilometers north of the city Vientiane. It is a structure of square bottle style with a height of 45 meters.

万象塔銮（邑石网供图）

The compound was constructed in 737, but some people believe that it was built in the 3rd or 6th century. There are still some other people who hold the view that the king Asoka ordered the construction of the building 2000 years ago.

The compound was originally a small structure built on a block of square stone. The greater pagoda was built in 1566 on the basis of the smaller one by the King Setthathirath. It was heavily damaged and eventually left abandoned in the 18th century and was rebuilt in the 1930's to its original design. A sacred relic from the Buddha was buried underneath.

The main pagoda is 45 meters high, consisting of a conical base surrounded by 24 large lotus petals and the main body in the shape of square bottle. The base had two layers, the first of which is square-shaped with a length of 61.3 meters from east to west, 58.48 meters from north to south. Four small pagodas are erected at each of the four corners. At the center of each side is a prayer gate with stairs leading to the arched gates of the upper layer.

The second layer of the base is also square in shape with a side length of 48

万象塔銮夜景（邑石网供图）

meters, and has three levels. The outer level is comprised of many lotus petals and on the second level are hundreds of sema stones among which there are statues of Buddha. Arched gates lead to the third level that contains 30 small stupas which are 3.6 meters tall and have a small golden stupa inside.

Atop the glittering main body of the pagoda covered in gold leaf is its spire of complicated structure, consisting of the inverted-funnel-shape base, topped by two-tiered square platform, square lotus pedal, funnel-shaped square platform, round lotus pedal and precious bottle, the main part containing the two-tiered canopy, a precious bottle, another two canopies and precious bottle, and the spire top in the shape of a precious bead.

老挝琅勃拉邦普西塔

Luang Prabrang Phonsi Pagoda Laos

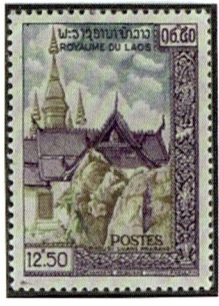

普西塔邮票（老挝 1959 年发行）

　　普西塔位于老挝琅勃拉邦城中的普西山，普西山高 100 多米，此山是琅勃拉邦的制高点，在山顶可浏览琅勃拉邦全城。

　　普西塔就建在山顶，此塔也就成了琅勃拉邦城的标志。

　　传说佛祖曾在普西山上留下了一个脚印，后人便在此处建佛塔以示纪念。普西塔形制类似塔銮，中心主塔为一方瓶形塔，四周配以几个宝伞和几座小塔。塔刹也是一宝伞。普西塔的中心主塔全身敷以金箔，是老挝北部著名佛塔。

　　Located on top of Mount Phou Si in the city Luang Prabrang, Laos, the pagoda is over 100 meters in height and is the commanding point and one of the major landmarks of the city. Legend has it that the Buddha used to leave a footprint on Mount Phou Si, and thus a pagoda was constructed here in honor of the event.

　　The compound resembles the Lao-style stupa, the main building of which is the structure in the shape of square bottle surrounded by a few precious umbrellas and small pagodas. The spire is also shaped as precious umbrella. The central pagoda covered in gold leaf is one of the famous monuments in northern Laos.

柬埔寨吴哥城巴戎寺佛塔群

Angkor Wat Bayon Temple Pagodas Cambodia

巴戎寺佛塔邮票（柬埔寨 1966 年发行）

笑面佛（邑石网供图）

巴戎寺佛塔群位于吴哥城的中心，为高棉式佛塔，建成于公元 1200 年左右。当时是阇耶跋摩七世国王当政，国王笃信佛教，巴戎寺是他主持修建的，该寺有 54 座大小宝塔。

巴戎寺各个建筑物之上，多建石质尖塔。尖塔是建在两层空心须弥座之上。所有尖塔呈圆锥形，用石块砌成，塔刹已不存。尖塔辟有圣龛，供奉佛像。

巴戎寺尖塔的四面都雕有巨大佛脸的佛面像。巴戎寺尖塔的四面佛面像，面容微笑，表情各异，安详中带有几分神秘。据说四面佛的四面分别代表"悲、喜、慈、舍"这四种境界。几十座佛面塔的微笑佛面极为特殊，"微笑高棉"由此而来。

巴戎寺的回廊有浅浮雕画面，浮雕画面的长度约 1200 米，雕刻约 11000 个人物。浮雕内容十分丰富，从王宫征战到平民生活应有尽有，都是佛教故事。

吴哥城的尖佛塔形似玉米棒。由于其形制的特殊性，被其他国家模仿，并被称作"高棉式佛塔"。

Located at Bayon Temple, the center of Angkor, Cambodia, the Khmer style pagodas were constructed in about 1200 A.D. during the reign of Jayavarman Ⅶ who was devoted to Buddhism and ordered the construction of Bayon Temple.

There are 54 pagodas of different sizes on top of the main buildings in the temple, most of which are made of stone and sit on the hollow two-tiered Sumeru pedestal. The stone pagodas are all cone-shaped without spires on the top, in which there are shrines dedicated to the Buddha.

All sides of the pagodas are carved with gigantic smiling faces of Buddha, different in expressions. It is supposed that the faces on the four sides represent sorrow, joy, kindness and sacrifice respectively. The smiling faces of Buddha on the dozens of pagodas are so impressive that it is where the "Smiling Khmer" came from.

The cloister walls of Bayon Temple are decorated with relief sculptures which are approximately 1200 meters in length and include more than 10 thousand figures displaying many Buddhist stories of the royal campaigns and the civilian lives.

Pagodas in Angkor, similar in shape to corns, are so special for their structure that they are imitated by other countries in the constructions of their pagodas, thus the name "Khmer Style Pagoda".

巴戎寺佛塔群(邑石网供图)

印度尼西亚婆罗浮屠佛塔群
Borobudur Indonesia

（老挝 1975 年发行）

婆罗浮屠邮票

（印度尼西亚 1994 年发行）

婆罗浮屠邮票

婆罗浮屠佛塔群位于印度尼西亚日惹市西北，佛塔建于公元 750—850 年间。

塔群通高 35 米，占地面积 1.23 万平方米。仅仅石料就耗用 5.5 万立方米。

佛塔群建在一个边长 120 米的两层方形折角塔基上，塔基边长 123 米，高 4 米。塔基上建方形十字折角须弥座。

婆罗浮屠佛塔的大须弥座有五层，各层面积向上逐层收缩。

须弥座第一层，距塔基边沿有 7 米。以上各层，每层都缩进 2 米，留下了狭长的走廊。

在大型须弥座之上，建有四层圆形佛塔群。最上面是一大型覆钵式佛塔，塔高 7 米，直径 9.9 米。除中央大塔外，还有三层小塔，共 72 座。各小塔也是覆钵式塔。各小塔塔身中空，外壁则留有规则的方孔，以减轻大风压力。

各塔塔顶是塔刹，大小塔塔刹形制相似。塔刹底层是方箱，其上则是一个六面锥形石柱。

婆罗浮屠各层须弥座的周边上面，也建有众多覆钵式小塔。各层须弥座的外立面上，辟有佛龛，内供佛像。上三层圆形平台上也雕有佛像，全塔共有佛像 504 尊。

在婆罗浮屠整个建筑的外立面和回廊上，布满了佛教故事的浮雕。各式浮雕约有 2670 块，总面积约 2500 平方米。

婆罗浮屠佛塔群自 10 世纪逐渐荒废，19 世纪初始被人发现，但佛塔已部分残破。公元 1973 年联合国教科文组织和印尼政府发起一项修复计划，即"抢救婆罗浮屠"计划，一些国家还为此发行邮票。工程竣工后，婆罗浮屠佛塔群被列入世界文化遗产名录。

Located about 40 kilometers northwest of Yogyakarta, Indonesia, Borobudur was constructed during the year 750 and 850. The compound is 35 meters in height, covering an area of 12 300 square meters. It is said that over 55 000 cubic meters of stone are used for its construction.

The compound is erected on a 2-layered base with a height of 4 meters and the side length of 123 meters. The large Sumeru pedestal is composed of five square terraces, each of diminishing height. The first terrace is set back 7 meters from the edge of the base. Each subsequent terrace is set back 2 meters, leaving a narrow

婆罗浮屠佛塔群（邑石网供图）

婆罗浮屠顶部塔群(邑石网供图)

corridor at each stage.

On the large Sumeru pedestal are four rows of pagodas arranged in concentric circles, the top of which is a large inverted-style structure, 7 meters tall and 9.9 meters in diameter. The other three rows include 72 small inverted-style pagodas, which are hollow inside and have square holes to relieve the pressure of strong wind.

The spires of the pagodas are similar in form, consisting of a base shaped like square platform and a six-sided tapered stone pillar.

There are 504 statues of Buddha on each terrace of circular platforms and in shrines on the exterior side of the Sumeru pedestal. The exterior side of the entire building and the cloister walls are decorated with a lot of relief sculptures of Buddhist stories, totaling 2670 pieces and covering an area around 2500 square meters.

Borobudur has been gradually abandoned since the 10th century and was discovered in the 19th century, but the pagodas are partially broken. In 1973, the UNESCO and the Indonesian government launched a rehabilitation program, called "the rescue of Borobudur", and some countries issued stamps featuring the compound. After the completion of the project, Borobudur was listed on the world cultural heritage list.

南传佛教地区的佛塔

汉传
佛教地区的佛塔

Pagodas in Han Buddhism Areas

北京天宁寺塔

Tianning Temple Pagoda Beijing

北京天宁寺塔邮票（冈比亚1993年发行）

　　北京天宁寺塔位于北京西城区广安门外，建于辽代天祚帝天庆九年（公元1119年）。塔高57.8米，是一座八角十三层密檐式实心砖塔。天宁寺塔的艺术成就，集中在基座和塔身第一层。

　　关于天宁寺塔的建造年代，以前没有明确记载。1991年对此塔大修时，在塔刹中发现一块辽代建塔碑。碑文明确记载此塔建于天庆九年至十年（公元1119—1120年）。

　　天宁寺塔的结构，由基台、塔座、塔身和塔刹组成。塔基台呈方形，前面有踏步台阶。塔座呈八面形，底部有两层素面台阶，其上也有两层，下层每面有六个龛，龛内雕狮子头。

天宁寺塔塔身第一层是塔的艺术精华所在。东、西、南、北四面设半圆形券门，券门两侧雕菩萨、力士。

券门内下部为格子门扇（北面为板门扇），券门内上部雕各组不同的主佛及菩萨。

天宁寺塔第一层的其他四面则设直棂窗，窗两侧雕菩萨像，窗顶部有两面雕菩萨像，另东南面雕普贤菩萨及其坐骑"獠蛮"，西南面雕文殊菩萨及其坐骑"拂林"。

塔身第二层及以上为十二层密檐，从下而上，逐层收减，每层塔檐下施仿木结构的砖雕斗拱。每个檐角挂有风铃。

天宁寺塔塔刹的底部是八角形素面刹座，其上是两层八角仰莲，上托小须弥座和三层相轮，再上是一巨大的宝珠。

Located outside Guang'anmen in Xicheng District, Beijing, Tianning Temple pagoda is built during the reign of Emperor Tianzuo of Liao dynasty. The thirteen-storey multi-eaved pagoda, 57.8 meters tall, is octagonal-based, entirely solid, and made of brick and stone. The artistic achievements of Tianning Temple pagoda are mainly displayed in pedestal and the first storey of its body. There was no clear and definite record as to the date of the construction of the pagoda. Yet, a stone tablet found in 1991 when the pagoda was repaired keeps a record that the pagoda was constructed in the years from 1119 to 1120.

Tianning Temple pagoda is composed of the platform, the pedestal, the body and the steeple. The platform is square with steps in the front. The pedestal of the pagoda is an octagonal structure and is divided into two levels. On the first level there are six niches on each side with lions' heads carved inside.

The first storey shows the artistic essence of the pagoda. On four sides of the first storey, facing the four directions, there are arched doorways with relief sculptures of Bodhisattva and Vagrapani on both sides.

The lower part of the doorway is lattice-shaped door leaf (plank door leaf to the

北京天宁寺塔（朱静阳摄影）

north). The upper part is carved with groups of different Buddhas and Bodhisattvas. On the other four sides of the first storey of the pagoda are vertical bar windows with Bodhisattva carved on both sides and two sculptures of Bodhisattva on the top of the windows. The relief sculptures of Samantabhadra and his white elephant mount are carved on the southeast side, and Manjusri riding on a blue lion on the southwest side.

The second storey and the upper storeys are in the style of 12 tiers of eaves diminishing in size as they progress upward. Under each tier is brick carving bracket supports imitating the wooden-constructed bracket. Aeolian bells are hang at every angle of the eaves.

The spire has an octagonal base at the bottom above which are two layers of lotus petals surmounted by a small Sumeru pedestal and 3 tiers of discs. The spire top is decorated with a huge precious bead .

北京香山琉璃塔

Fragrant Hill Glazed Pagoda Beijing

（柬埔寨1999年发行）

香山琉璃塔邮票

（加纳1996年发行）

香山琉璃塔邮票

　　北京香山琉璃塔位于北京香山公园内，建于清代乾隆四十五年（公元1780年），是为迎接六世班禅进京而修建的。

　　塔高40米，是一座八角七层楼阁式实心琉璃塔。琉璃塔下为石砌方形基台，其上建八角形基座。基座周围施白玉栏杆，栏杆内建木构附阶，附阶呈八角形，其形特别宽大，这是此塔的特点。

　　香山琉璃塔塔身为实心体。各层均用黄、绿、紫、蓝各色琉璃构件，砌成塔身的柱子、拱门、额枋等。在层间砌成斗拱、檐椽和瓦垄，成为塔檐。各层每面的拱门内，端坐琉璃佛像。

　　香山琉璃塔底层附阶的顶部建八角形屋面，屋面收作八角形平台，平台周边绕以白玉栏杆，此平台成为佛塔二层的基座。

　　琉璃塔塔刹底部是刹座，顶部是一巨大的琉璃宝珠。

香山琉璃塔（朱静阳摄影）

Located in the Fragrant Hill Park, Beijing, the glazed pagoda was built in 1780 during the reign of Qianlong Emperor especially for the accommodation of the Sixth Panchen Lama when he went to Beijing from Tibet. The pagoda is octagonal-shaped, 40 meters tall, and has seven storeys adorned with glazed tiles.

At the bottom of the glazed pagoda are an octagonal platform and a stone square pedestal to support the main structure. In the middle of the stone base, surrounded by white marble balustrades, is the pavilion-style building, the pent roof of which is supported by wooden columns.

The body of the glazed pagoda is solid, and every storey is composed of yellow, green, purple, blue and other colorful glazed parts, such as the pillars, arched doors, architrave, brackets, beams and ridge tiles. A bronze bell hangs at every angle of the eaves, and glazed statues of Buddha sit in the arched doors of all sides of each storey.

The spire has a base at the bottom and is crowned by a huge precious bead.

北京颐和园多宝琉璃塔

Duobao Glazed Pagoda Beijing

颐和园多宝琉璃塔邮票（柬埔寨 1999 年发行）

　　颐和园多宝琉璃塔位于北京颐和园万寿山的后山，塔身坐南向北。该塔建于乾隆十六年（公元 1751 年），是为庆祝皇太后六十寿辰而建。多宝琉璃塔塔高 16 米，为不等边八角形，七级，是一座楼阁式和密檐式相结合的塔。

　　多宝琉璃塔塔檐的第二、四、六、七层，层间很小，类似密檐。塔的第一、三、五各层塔檐之间塔身较长，是楼阁式类型。

　　第二层塔檐之上是须弥座和汉白玉栏杆，上建第三层塔身。第四层塔檐之上也是须弥座，上建第五层。

　　在塔身的四个正面，设拱券形大佛龛，内坐琉璃佛像。在大佛龛周围布满一排排小佛龛，龛内坐小佛像。在塔的第一、三、五各层塔身的四个斜面也布满小佛龛，内坐小佛像。

　　多宝琉璃塔的塔刹较为特殊。刹座之上为华盖，华盖之上是法铃，这是一个铃铛形法器，再往上是圆光装饰物和宝珠。

Located at the back of Longevity Hill inside the Summer Palace of Beijing, Duobao Glazed Pagoda, sitting northward, was built in 1751 during the reign of Qianlong Emperor of Qing dynasty to celebrate the 60th birthday of Empress Dowager.

Duobao Glazed Pagoda, inequilaterally octagonal-shaped, is 16 meters high and has seven storeys. It is a combination of pavilion-style and multi-eaved style. The space between the layers of eaves of the second, fourth, sixth and seventh storeys is narrow, which makes these parts look like a multi-eaved structure. By contrast, the space between the layers of eaves of the first, third and fifth storeys are wide, so these parts take on a pavilion style.

The Sumeru pedestal with white marble balustrades is built on the eaves of

多宝琉璃塔上部（朱静阳摄影）

多宝琉璃塔（朱静阳摄影）

汉传佛教地区的佛塔

the second storey topped with the body of the third storey. There are also Sumeru pedestals on the eaves of the fourth storey topped with the body of the fifth storey.

Huge arched niches with glazed statue of the Buddha can be seen on the front of four sides of the pagoda. The huge niches are surrounded by rows of small niches with small statues of Buddha inside. The four sides of the first, third and fifth storeys are also covered with many small niches housing small statues of Buddha.

The pagoda has a particularly different spire. On the bottom of the spire is a canopy, with bronze bells hanging at its sides. There is a bell-shaped ritual instrument on the canopy and a halo-like decoration unit crowned by a precious bead.

北京通州燃灯塔

Randeng Pagoda Beijing

通州燃灯塔邮票（柬埔寨 1999 年发行）

通州燃灯塔位于北京通州区北运河岸边。始建于北周末期（公元 577—581 年），塔高 56 米，是一座八角十三层实心砖木结构的密檐式塔。

燃灯塔始建于北周末期。唐贞观七年（公元 633 年）复建，辽重熙年间（公元 1032—1054 年）重建。

燃灯塔的基座为八角形须弥座。塔身的第一层较为简约，正南面辟券门，内供燃灯佛，其余三正面设假门，其他四斜面设假窗。燃灯塔全塔有 2000 多颗铜风铃。檐角挂两枚，椽头挂一枚。

通州燃灯塔在清康熙十八年（公元 1679 年）遭地震，佛塔震倒，只余塔座，康熙三十七年（公元 1698 年）复建。八国联军入侵时，塔遭枪击，部分受损。1976 年唐山地震，波及此塔，幸未倾圮，但塔顶受损。1985—1987 年重建塔顶及塔刹。

康熙十八年（公元 1679 年）地震，塔身倾圮，有人发现一颗佛牙舍利，还有数百粒其他舍利，当时重修塔身时，此舍利已入藏天宫。但公元 1985 年重修塔顶时，在塔的顶层和塔刹内并未发现舍利。

通州燃灯塔（朱静阳摄影）

燃灯塔的塔刹极其壮美。塔刹底部是八角素底座，其上是两层莲花台，再上有三层莲瓣。

塔刹中央嵌一根铁制刹心柱，柱上串接着各种法器。最下面是空心宝珠，直径 2.25 米，上面饰古钱纹和卷草纹。

宝珠内由四条扁钢支撑，扁钢上面还有三条铭文，其中一条铭文是"康熙岁次戊寅仲夏旦立"，另一条铭文是"成造宝塔戒僧赵盛修建"，再一条铭文是"成造解进忠"。

空心宝珠之上是五层相轮，再上是圆光、仰月和四联宝珠。

Located on the bank of the Canal, the pagoda, made of brick and wood, octagonal, thirteen-eaved solid structure, is 56 meters high and is a typical example of multi-eaved pavilion-style.

The pagoda was first built at the end of North Zhou dynasty, and reconstructed in Tang dynasty and Liao dynasty.

Randeng Pagoda is seated on a Sumeru pedestal. The first storey is particularly tall with simple decorations. The southern door is open and a statue of Buddha is enshrined inside. The other three doors are purely ornamental. False windows decorate the other four sides of the first storey.

More than two thousand bells are hung all over the pagoda, two bells at each angle of the eaves and one at each rafter end.

The pagoda was ruined by an earthquake in 1679 during the reign of Kangxi Emperor of Qing dynasty. The main body of the pagoda fell apart and the only remaining part was its base. Later the pagoda was rebuilt in 1698. The pagoda was damaged again by gunshots during the invasion of eight-nation alliance. The top of the pagoda was destroyed because of another earthquake in 1976 and a repair was made to its top and spire from1985 to 1987.

When the pagoda fell down in 1679, hundreds of relics were found and later were said to be put back into the upper parts of the pagoda when the building was renovated. But when the pagoda was being repaired again in 1985, those relics were not found in the top storey and the spire.

The spire of the pagoda is especially magnificent and beautiful. Its pedestal is in the shape of octagon, and two layers of lotus stages and three layers of blooming lotus petals rest on it. The central pole is made of metal and various ritual instruments are attached to it. A hollow precious bead, 2.25 meters in diameter is at the lower end. The four flat steels supporting the huge bead inside are carved with some inscriptions. Atop the hollow bead are the five-tiered discs, the halo, the moon and four smaller precious beads.

北京房山云居寺北塔
Yunju Temple North Pagoda Beijing

房山云居寺北塔邮票（柬埔寨 1999 年发行）

房山云居寺北塔位于北京市房山区云居寺。建于辽代。北塔通高 34.2 米。

关于此塔的建造年代，说法不一。就其两层楼阁式部分，应是隋唐时期的产物，在辽代重熙年间重建成现塔模样。

云居寺北塔其实是一座有巨大塔刹的楼阁式塔。下为八角形须弥座，上建两层楼阁塔，其上为塔刹。

北塔塔身八面分设拱门和隐形直棂窗。塔身内有梯道。在基座上有砖雕的技乐天、反弹琵琶、人面鸟身等。

北塔塔刹底部是刹座，之上是覆钵、相轮、覆钟、莲台、宝瓶、多层莲瓣，顶部为宝珠。此塔塔刹底部为覆钵，其形如鼓，相轮之上为覆钟。由于有鼓有钟，有人把此塔称为钟鼓楼式塔。

Located in Yunju temple, Fangshan District, Beijing, the North Pagoda was built in Liao dynasty. It measures 34.2 meters in height.

There is no agreement as to the time when it was built. Judging from its architectural and artistic style, it may be a product of Sui and Tang dynasty and the present building is the original structure when it was rebuilt in Liao dynasty.

The North Pagoda is a pavilion style pagoda with a Sumeru pedestal at the bottom, on which stands the two-storey main body topped with a huge spire.

The eight sides of the pagoda are decorated with arched doors and mullion windows. The interior structure of the pagoda is a central pillar with a winding staircase, both made of bricks. The base of the pagoda is decorated with beautiful designs of brick carvings.

The spire of the pagoda consists of several parts including the pedestal, inverted bowl, discs, inverted bell, lotus seat, precious bottle, blooming lotus petals topped with a precious bead. The spire pedestal is in the shape of a drum-like inverted bowl and on the discs there is an inverted bell. The pagoda is thus classified into bell and drum style pagodas.

河北定州料敌塔

Liaodi Pagoda Hebei Province

定州料敌塔邮票（加纳 1996 年发行）

　　定州料敌塔位于河北定州市南门内。始建于北宋咸平四年（公元 1001 年），建成于至和二年（公元 1055 年）。料敌塔塔高 84.2 米，是国内第一高塔。基座直径约 25 米，是一座八角十一层砖砌楼阁塔。

　　料敌塔是宋真宗为了奉安寺僧取回的舍利和经卷下诏修建的，建塔历时 55 年。当地有"砍尽嘉山木，修成定县塔"之说。

　　料敌塔结构是由基座、塔身和塔刹组成。结构为双层砖套筒。

　　塔内有塔梯可通塔顶，并与塔身四门相通。定州料敌塔内两壁间有佛龛，塔壁有精细花纹雕刻和生动彩画。各层廊壁多历代碑刻和名人题咏。各层假窗浮雕几何纹窗棂。

　　由于地震的影响，料敌塔的东北角在光绪十年（公元 1884 年）从上至下突然塌落。塌落的是塔的外壁，露出塔的塔心柱，而塔的其他外壁依然完好，从其他方向看，佛塔像是完好的塔。这座残损的塔，依然挺立了 100 多年。直到公元 1988 年，中央拨专款对塔身进行修复并完好如初。

　　料敌塔塔刹下为刹座，其上为大忍冬花叶，再上是覆钵，覆钵之上是承露盘，再上是两枚青铜宝珠。

Located inside the southern gate of the ancient city of Dingzhou, Hebei province, Liaodi Pagoda was first constructed during Northern Song dynasty and completed in 1055. Liaodi Pagoda is octagonal, 84.2 meters high, and is the tallest of all extant ancient pagodas in China. The brick pagoda is in pavilion-style and has eleven storeys.

During Northern Song dynasty a Buddhist monk went on a pilgrimage to

定州开元寺料敌塔附近(朱静阳摄影)

古建专家罗哲文为料敌塔题写"中华第一塔"（朱静阳摄影）

India for Buddhist scriptures. Upon his return Emperor Zhenzong issued a decree for the construction of a pagoda to house the scriptures and Buddhist relics. The construction of the building lasted 55 years. It is said that the woods in the Jiashan mountain were almost wiped out in order to build the pagoda.

The pagoda is composed of the base, the body and the spire. The storeys are well proportioned, giving the pagoda a lofty and elegant appearance. Doors were installed on four sides of each storey and false windows on the other four sides. The first storey is relatively high, with a balcony and eaves. Inside the pagoda a winding staircase in the middle leads to the upper levels. The short eaves were built by stacking tier upon tier of bricks around the body of the pagoda. The other storeys have eaves but no balconies.

There are shrines for statue of Buddha between the walls decorated with exquisite carved patterns and colorful paintings. Tablet inscriptions and words of some famous people of the past dynasties can be seen on the walls of the storeys. The windows are ornamented with geometric patterns.

The pagoda was damaged by an earthquake in 1884. The remaining parts had been there for more than 100 years. Special fund was allotted by the central government to restore it to its original appearance in 1988.

The pagoda spire is composed of a subbase decorated with large honeysuckle leaves, an inverted—bowl—shaped top, an iron disc and a pair of bronze beads.

河南登封法王寺舍利塔

Fawang Temple Pagoda Henan Province

（中国 1995 年发行）登封法王寺舍利塔邮票

（冈比亚 1993 年发行）登封法王寺舍利塔邮票

　　登封法王寺舍利塔位于登封法王寺后面小山坡上。始建于隋代仁寿二年（公元 602 年）。舍利塔是一座方形十五级密檐式砖塔。

　　法王寺舍利塔不但历史悠久，且景色甚佳，被称为"嵩山第一胜地"，有名的中岳八景之一"嵩门待月"就在此地。

　　舍利塔高 34.18 米，底层周长 28 米，底层高 11.08 米。各层施叠涩出檐，出檐最宽处达 0.9 米。

　　塔身外轮廓呈抛物线状，七层以上塔身急剧收小，与嵩岳寺塔极为相似。

　　登封法王寺舍利塔的底层南面开一券门，内供白玉佛一尊。该玉佛是明永乐七年（公元 1409 年）9 月，周王为生子所送。年代已久，所供白玉佛的右下角和双手也已残损。

　　法王寺塔塔心为中空方形，塔内东西内壁靠近南端均有等距方形孔眼，用以插方木（现仍有 9 根），据推测可能是为安装塔梯之用。

　　舍利塔年岁已久，已有残损。塔身向西倾斜 35 厘米，南面塔壁顺着各

登封法王寺舍利塔（燕岊宇摄影）

层券窗有开裂的通裂缝。塔身下部的塔檐四角崩坏或位移，上部塔砖风化、脱落。

塔刹已残，现仅存仰莲、宝盖。

塔底层塔壁外面，距地面 5.5 至 8.65 米之间，每面均凿有两列三层方孔。可能原先塔外建有外廊或其他附属建筑。

Located in Fawang Temple five kilometers northwest of the county town of Dengfeng at the foot of Yuzhu Peak of Mount Song，the pagoda was first built in 602，Sui dynasty. The square pagoda has 15 layers of eaves and is made of bricks.

The pagoda is 34.18 meters tall. The perimeter of its first storey is 28 meters and its height is 11.08 meters. The eaves of each storey were built by stacking tier upon tier of bricks around the body of the pagoda and the widest eaves measure 90 centimeters. An arched door is made on the south side of the first storey，inside which there is a shrine for a jade statue of Buddha presented by the king of Luoyang in 1409 in Ming dynasty. As time went by，the lower right part and the hands of the statue have been worn out.

The inner part of the pagoda is square and hollow. The east and west walls inside the pagoda are punched with square holes holding the square timbers (9 timbers remaining) for the purpose of installing the staircase.

The spire has been ruined，with only lotus petals and canopy left.

The pagoda has undergone some damages since it was built. The body is leaning westward by 35 centimeters and penetrating cracks can be seen on the walls of each storey. The eaves of the lower part of the pagoda have been damaged or displaced and some bricks of the upper part have been weathered or have fallen off.

The outer sides of the walls at the lower part，5.5 to 8.65 meters above the ground，are punched with rows of square holes，from which it may be supposed that there used to be other attached buildings around the pagoda.

河南登封嵩岳寺塔
Songyue Temple Pagoda Henan Province

（中国 1958 年发行）
登封嵩岳寺塔邮票

（冈比亚 1993 年发行）
登封嵩岳寺塔邮票

　　登封嵩岳寺塔位于登封市西北大室山嵩岳寺内。建于北魏正光元年（公元 520 年）。塔高 41 米，为十二边形十五层密檐砖塔。

　　佛塔的建造是在北魏时代。北魏宣武帝元恪及其母胡太后崇尚佛法，欲在嵩山营造东土雷音，作为其拜佛诵经的道场。

　　宣武帝遂命使用京城洛阳河南郡三年财政收入，建造闲居寺舍利塔。至孝明帝正光元年（公元 520 年）建成。闲居寺在隋文帝仁寿元年（公元 601 年）改为嵩岳寺，舍利塔也改称嵩岳寺塔。

　　登封嵩岳寺塔由台基、塔身和宝刹组成。台基为十二边形，高 0.85 米，宽 16 米。前有月台，后有通道。

　　嵩岳寺塔身施密檐，檐间短壁每面各砌一门二窗，少数为真门窗，多数为假门窗。整体外轮廓呈柔和曲线形。

　　嵩岳寺塔内部为一中空筒。佛塔内无塔梯，外无塔棚，不能登临。据传原先都有，后世被火焚毁。

　　整个嵩岳寺塔使用薄青砖砌筑，用糯米汤拌黄泥做黏合剂。历经千年而不坏，屡遭地震而不倒。

　　嵩岳寺塔刹高 3.5 米，在刹座上置复莲、覆钵、仰莲，再砌纺锤形七重相轮和宝珠。

　　整个塔刹先用砖砌成毛坯，再雕琢成形。

　　1989 年在嵩岳寺塔的塔刹内发现两座天宫，分别位于宝珠和相轮中。天宫中出土银塔、瓷瓶、舍利罐和舍利子等。

　　嵩岳寺塔下有地宫，1988 年对地宫进行了发掘，发现文物 70 余件，其中人物造像 12 件，余为建筑构件等。

Located in Songyue Temple，Dengfeng County，Henan province，the Pagoda was built in 520，North Wei dynasty. The dodecagonal multi-eaved pagoda is 41 meters tall and has 15 storeys.

The pagoda was ordered to be constructed by Emperor Xuanwu. The Emperor and his mother thought highly of Buddhism and intended to bulid a temple on Songshan Mountain to worship Buddha.

With the three years' revenues of the capital city Luoyang，the temple，originally known as Xianju Temple，was ordered to be built. The construction was completed in 520. During the reign of Emperor Wendi in Sui dynasty，the temple was renamed Songyue Temple，and thus the pagoda got its present namc.

The pagoda is composed of the base，the body and the spire. The base is dodecagonal，85 centimeters high and 16 meters wide. There is a platform in the front and a passway at the back.

The pagoda is multi-eaved and there is a door and two windows on each side of the wall，most of which are ornamental. The exterior of the entire pagoda presents the contour of a smooth parabola.

The interior of the pagoda is cylindrical and hollow inside. There is neither staircases inside nor pylons outside to make people climb the pagoda. But it is said that the staircases and the pylons were available initially but were completely destroyed by a fire later.

The whole pagoda is made of thin black bricks and use glutinous rice soup

登封嵩岳寺塔（燕峘宇摄影）

mixed with mud as adhesive, and therefore the building survived more than a thousand years and many earthquakes.

The spire is 3.5 meters high and its pedestal is topped with lotus flower, inverted bowl, seven-tier discs, and a huge bead. It was first made with bricks and was roughly shaped, and then it was polished into its present form.

Two heavenly palaces were found inside the spire, in precious bead and discs respectively, from which some treasures such as a silver pagoda, porcelain bottles, and a pot containing relics are unearthed.

There is an underground palace under the pagoda. It was excavated in 1988 and more than seventy pieces of historical treasures were discovered including twelve figure statues and some building elements.

河南开封祐国寺铁塔

Youguo Temple Iron Pagoda Henan Province

开封铁塔邮票（中国 1994 年发行）

　　开封祐国寺（开宝寺）塔，俗称铁塔。位于开封铁塔公园内。建于宋仁宗皇祐元年（公元 1049 年）。铁塔为八面十三层楼阁式砖塔，高 55.88 米。

　　因为祐国寺塔的塔身镶嵌褐色琉璃砖，远看似铁色，故称铁塔。铁塔所在的祐国寺已不存在，现铁塔所在处辟为公园。

　　祐国寺塔是为供奉佛祖舍利而建。据说舍利来自印度阿育王，最先供奉于宁波阿育王寺。五代时吴越王钱俶将舍利迎入杭州罗汉寺，后吴越王降宋，佛舍利被迎入东京汴梁，供于大内滋福殿。公元 982 年宋太宗赵光义诏令建舍利塔，以供奉佛舍利，前后历经 8 年，于宋太宗端拱二年（公元 989 年）建成。

　　宋仁宗皇祐元年（公元 1049 年）诏令重建灵感塔供奉舍利。此次重建改木为砖，砖塔建成后，赐名开宝寺塔。其后宋英宗将开宝寺改为祐国寺，佛塔也改为祐国寺塔。

　　铁塔的建造极其精密浩繁。铁塔塔身外层全部镶嵌各种形状各种图案的琉璃砖，计有 50 多种。有人物砖、动物砖、花卉砖及装饰花纹砖等。

整个塔身是用28种不同形状的结构砖组合而成。在柱、斗拱、枋等需要咬合的部位，都是用特别烧制的有榫、有卯的子母砖紧紧扣合在一起的。

铁塔的底层，东西南北四面各开一门，其中北门通塔内，有塔梯可登塔，其余三个门内只有八角形小室。二层以上东西南北四面也各开一门，不过每层只有一个门是通透的，内通梯道，外通塔外，其余三个门是不通透的。

由于设计合理、结构紧密，历经多次地震、水患，铁塔巍然屹立。1938年日本侵略者发炮七八十发，炮击铁塔，使铁塔严重损坏，第八、第九层的外壁被打穿，留下两米大的洞，然铁塔仍傲然而立。

铁塔塔刹的底为一圆形刹座，座上安置铜质宝珠，宝珠由八根链条与塔顶的八角相连。

塔内的梯道依顺时针方向盘旋而上。梯道狭窄，只容一人上下。

每上一层都会有通透门，门外端设铁栏杆，人们可眺望塔外景色。

黄河干流就在铁塔附近，因黄河泛滥，塔的基座已埋入地下。河床高

祐国寺铁塔周围（燕岷宇摄影）

出铁塔地面 13 米，因此可以说，铁塔是在一条悬河之旁。

Located in Iron Park， Kaifeng city， Henan province， Youguo Temple Pagoda， known as the Iron Pagoda， was built in 1049 during the reign of Renzong Emperor， Song dynasty. The octagonal brick pagoda is 55.88 meters tall and is in pavilion style with 13 storeys.

The pagoda got the current name because of its outer walls paved with brown colored glazes， which makes it look like iron structure from the outside. The temple where the pagoda stands no longer exists， and the place today has become a park named after the Iron Pagoda.

The construction of Iron Pagoda is considered to be related to sarira. It is said that the sariras of Buddha Sakya were preserved by King Asoka. Asoka first ensconced the sariras by storing them in King Asoka temple of Ningbo city， and later the King of Wuyue moved them into another temple of Hangzhou. After the Wuyue State was brought to an end， the sariras were taken to Bianliang， the capital city of Northern Song dynasty and kept in the palace of the Emperor.

In the year 982， Taizong， Emperor of Northern Song dynasty ordered to build a pagoda to enshrine the sariras. The construction of the pagoda lasted for eight years and was completed in 989.

Renzong Emperor of Song dynasty ordered to rebuild the pagoda in 1049. The newly built structure was made of bricks and named Kaibao Temple Pagoda. Yingzong Emperor renamed the temple as Youguo Temple afterwards， and thus the pagoda got its present name called Youguo Temple Pagoda.

The construction of the iron pagoda is made in extreme precision and delicacy. There is a spire on its top and a palace underground. The body of the pagoda is made of bricks of 28 different shapes. Tenons are especially baked to join the components like pillars， brackets and tiebeams. The pagoda has doors on four sides， but people can approach the pagoda only by the steps on the north side. Thanks to the sensible and precise design， the iron pagoda remains intact after weathering many earthquake and floods in history.

The spire has a round pedestal topped with a bronze bead that is connected

祐国寺铁塔雨中倒影（燕岷宇摄影）

with eight corners of the roof by eight chains. There is an inner clockwise spiral stone staircase leading to the upper storeys，but the stairway is so narrow that it allows only one person to go up. People can go through the doors surrounded with iron railings outside and overlook the scenery on each storey of the pagoda.

　　The main stream of Yellow River runs near the pagoda. Because Yellow River used to overflow its banks in the past，the foundation of the pagoda has sunk into the silt of the river. The riverbed is 13 meters higher than the ground，and as it were，the pagoda is right beside a suspended river.

山西洪赵飞虹塔

Feihong Pagoda Shanxi Province

洪赵飞虹塔邮票（中国 1958 年发行）

  洪赵飞虹塔位于山西洪洞县广胜寺内。始建于东汉，原名霍山阿育王塔。明正德年间，因年久失修，广胜寺达连和尚立誓新修此塔。他募化四方，并得到官方资助，从明正德十年（公元 1515 年）到嘉靖元年（公元 1522 年），历时 12 年落成。因达连大师法号"飞虹"，遂改名飞虹塔。

  飞虹塔为八角十三层楼阁式塔，通高 47.31 米。塔身用青砖砌成，底层有木质回廊。二层以上塔身全部镶嵌琉璃件，但这不是普通琉璃瓦，而是有艺术造型的琉璃构件，且各构件由整体烧成。

  塔身第三层到第十层都辟有佛龛、门洞，内置佛像、菩萨、童子像等琉璃件。门洞两侧均镶嵌琉璃盘龙、宝珠等。

  飞虹塔内有曲曲折折的塔梯，不断翻转身体可攀登至第十层。塔身从下到上收分很大，重心稳定。经多次地震，特别是经历康熙三十四年（公元 1696 年）临汾八级大地震，飞虹塔仍傲然挺立。

  飞虹塔的重要特点是二、三、四层的艺术造型图案。各层各个面都是一组一组的，每一层每一面都是一组完整的造型画面。

在各幅图案中嵌有佛像、菩萨、天王、金刚力士、盘龙、凤凰、狮子、大象、植物花卉等琉璃件。

整个塔身外部的琉璃装饰五彩斑斓、色泽如新。整座塔就是一幅艺术品。

飞虹塔的塔刹，是金刚宝座式，共有五座小塔，中间之塔稍大，四边四个很小的塔。

中间之塔，底为覆钵座，上为宝盖，宝盖上是宝珠，再上是仰莲，仰莲之上是葫芦状双宝珠。为确保安全，在宝珠上拴八条铁链系在塔顶八个

洪赵飞虹塔（秦槐健摄影）

檐角上。

Located in Guangsheng Temple, Hongdong county of Shanxi province, Feihong Pagoda, initially known as Huoshan King Asoka Pagoda, was first built in East Han dynasty. In Ming dynasty, a monk of Guangsheng Temple, whose monastic name was Feihong, decided to rebuild the pagoda, for it went to decay and in a state of disrepair, and he tried hard to collect alms and ask for the official fund. The pagoda had been constructed for 12 years and was renamed after the monk.

This octagonal-base structure stands at a current height of 47.31 meters, with 13 storeys. It is a solid-core brick building with wooden winding corridor on the first storey. The outside of the upper storeys of the pagoda is paved with glazed components decorated with delicate patterns.

There are niches, from the third to the tenth storey, in which glazed statues of Buddha, Bodhisattva, and statue of boys are placed. Both sides of door openings are decorated with glazed dragon and beads.

There is a winding staircase leading to the tenth storey. The pagoda is so articulated and firm that it survived many severe earthquakes.

The pagoda features intricate and richly detailed carvings. The walls of the second, the third and the fourth storey are decorated with groups of artistic designs, each forming a complete picture. Among them there are glazed components including Buddha, Bodhisattva, dragon, phoenix, lion, elephant, and various plants and flowers. The exterior features different varieties of colorful and shining glazed brick. The pagoda can be seen as a masterpiece of pagoda architecture.

The spire is in Sumeru style containing 5 small pagodas, the middle one of which is bigger than the other four. The pedestal of the middle pagoda is in the shape of inverted-bowl topped with a canopy, a precious bead, and lotus flower. Eight chains from the bead are connected with eight corners of the roof for the sake of safety.

山西释迦塔

Sakyamumi Pagoda Shanxi Province

释迦塔邮票（中国 1958 年发行）

释迦塔位于山西应县城内西北佛宫寺内，建于辽清宁二年（公元 1056
年），为八面五层楼阁式塔。

释迦塔本名佛宫寺塔，为纯木结构，不用金属件，故俗称应县木塔。

木塔塔高 67.31 米，底层直径 30.27 米。第一层为重檐，其他各层为单
檐，实际是五层六檐。各层间设有暗层，内部实为九层。

木塔是建在 4 米高的石砌台基之上。木塔是用内外两圈大柱支撑，外
圈用 24 根柱子，内圈用 8 根柱子。木柱之间用许多斜撑组成不同方向的木
架。

木塔底层南北各开一门，二至五层，各开四门。各层均设木隔窗，光
线充足，二层以上设平座栏杆，并可眺览风景。塔内装有木梯，可以登临。

木塔每层檐角挂有风铃。木塔内各层塑有佛像。

木塔文化内容丰富，塔内外名人所题匾额有 74 块。其中明成祖朱棣在
永乐四年（公元 1406 年）所题"峻极神工"匾额。明武宗朱厚照在正德
三年（公元 1508 年）所题"天下奇观"匾额。

塔内收藏经卷甚多。不久前发现在大佛体内珍藏银盒两只，内藏七宝和佛牙舍利。经证实是佛祖真身舍利，是木塔镇塔之宝。

木塔顶部为塔刹，塔刹高 9.91 米。刹座是八角素面座和两层仰莲。仰莲之上为宝瓶，五重相轮。刹顶为圆光、仰月、双宝珠、宝盖和另一组宝珠。这是一组完美的塔刹。

The Sakyamuni Pagoda is located in Fogong (Buddha's Palace) Temple in the northwestern corner of Yingxian county. Built in 1056, the 2nd year of Qingning reign, the octagonal pagoda has five storeys and is in pavilion style. The pagoda is originally named Fogong Temple Pagoda. Since it was built completely of timber, without any metal components, it has been known popularly as the Wooden Pagoda of Yingxian County.

应县木塔（秦槐键摄影）

Standing 67.31 meters high, 30.27 meters in diameter at its bottom, the pagoda has 9 storeys including the built-in storeys; outwards, there are 5 storeys and 6 eaves—the first storey with double eaves and the other 5 with single eave respectively between every two storeys.

The pagoda was constructed on a 4-meter-high stone platform, supported by two circles of wooden poles, 8 inside and 24 outside, among poles are many wooden girders, beams, and columns. There are two gates in both south and north at the ground storey, four gates from the second storey above. Each storey has windows allowing adequate light in and there are also balconies with banisters around the second storey and the upper storeys, so people can have a clear view. A wooden staircase is available inside the pagoda, leading up to the upper storeys. Wind bells hang under the eaves, and there are sculptures of Buddha on each storey.

The Wooden Pagoda has a rich collection of cultural objects including 74 inscriptions by the celebrities of the past dynasties, from home and abroad, among which there are one entitled in 1406 by Zhu Di, the third emperor of Ming dynasty, and one given in 1508 by Zhu Houzhao, the tenth emperor of Ming dynasty. In addition, there are many sutras and Buddhist relics which have been proved to be real relics of Buddha and has become the most valuable part of the pagoda.

The spire of the pagoda is 9.91 meters tall with an octagonal base, on which there are two tiers of lotus petals, precious bottle, two-layer discs, circular polarization, crescent moon, two precious beads, canopy and another group of beads. The sophisticated structure of the spire makes the utmost of ancient architecture techniques.

陕西延安宝塔

Yan'an Pagoda Shaanxi Province

（中国1946年发行）
延安宝塔邮票

（中国1964年发行）
延安宝塔邮票

　　延安宝塔亦称岭山寺塔，位于延安宝塔山（古称嘉岭山）上。始建于唐，岭山寺早已不存，现塔为明代建筑。宝塔高44米，八角九层楼阁式砖塔，塔内有梯可达塔顶。塔刹已不存。

　　关于延安造塔的缘由，有几种传说。有一说此处曾有两条恶龙，为害乡里。玉皇大帝遂派众神下凡建"镇邪塔"，塔身九级，内置一金人，两恶龙被金人所缚。佛塔镇龙治水，有点靠谱。

　　塔底层有二拱门，一门额题"高超碧落"，一门额题"俯视红尘"。

　　滚滚延河水，巍巍宝塔山。"延河水清清，宝塔高入云。"

　　宝塔是革命圣地延安的象征，是革命和进步的象征。曾几何时，有多少进步青年和民主人士，千里迢迢奔赴延安。而现在这里也是红色旅游胜地。

　　宝塔旁有一口大钟，据说是明崇祯年间铸造，曾以此报警。"巍巍宝塔据雄岗，八面凌霄八面窗。雄镇榆林依古镇，浮屠高崎射天狼。"在古代，宝塔曾是军事重地。

Located on top of the Pagoda Hill, Yan'an city in North Shaanxi, the pagoda, also known as Lingshan Temple Pagoda, was first built in Tang dynasty. The temple no longer exists and the residual pagoda is the construction of Ming dynasty.

There are two arched doors on the ground storey with an inscription above each doorframe.

The pagoda used to be an important place for military purpose, and is the symbol of Yan'an City, the holy land of Chinese revolution. Quite a number of enlightened young people and democrats traveled a long distance to get there not long ago. Today, it is one of the world-renowned holy land of "Red Tourism".

延安宝塔周围（秦槐键摄影）

延安宝塔（秦槐键摄影）

There are several different legends as to the construction of Yan'an Pagoda. One reliable legend goes that there were two evil dragons in this area that did great damage to the place and the native people. The Jade Emperor (the Supreme Deity of Taoism) had to send his follower gods to build a pagoda to repress the dragons. The pagoda has nine storeys with a gold man inside, who is said to have caught the evil dragons and thus the area is free from floods.

陕西长安玄奘墓塔

Xuanzang Tomb Pagoda Shaanxi Province

玄奘墓塔邮票（冈比亚 1973 年发行）

长安玄奘墓塔位于西安市长安区兴教寺，建于唐总章二年（公元 669 年）。玄奘法师于公元 664 年在今陕西省宜君县玉华宫圆寂（玉华宫现属铜川市印台区），依玄奘遗言"择山间僻处安置，勿近宫寺"，后人将其葬于西安浐河东岸白鹿原，公元 669 年迁葬于兴教寺并建墓塔。

玄奘法师（公元 602—664 年），俗名陈祎，洛阳缑氏人（今河南偃师境内）。

他于唐贞观二年（公元 628 年）从长安出发，经四年到达印度那烂陀寺，拜名僧戒贤为师。他学识优异，誉满全印。贞观十七年（公元 643 年）玄奘开始回国，于贞观十九年（公元 645 年）携大量经卷回到长安。

回到长安后他先后译出经、论 75 部，凡 1335 卷，并把《老子》和《大乘起信论》译成梵文，传入印度。由玄奘法师口述，其门徒辩机记录的长达十二卷的《大唐西域记》传世。

玄奘墓塔为方形五层楼阁式砖塔，塔高 23 米，底边长 5.2 米，坐北面南。墓塔底层南面辟砖砌拱门，内有方室，供奉玄奘塑像。底层北面镶嵌

玄奘法师墓塔（朱静玥摄影）

石刻《大唐三藏大遍觉法师塔铭并序》碑。

　　塔南面门额上方刻有"唐三藏墖"塔名，塔门两侧镌有楹联一副，上联为"造塔功德愿众生"，下联为"发菩提心同成佛"。塔的二层以上为实心，不能登临。

　　玄奘墓塔的两侧为二弟子灵塔，东边一座是玄奘弟子窥基灵塔，西边一座是玄奘弟子圆测灵塔。两塔均为方形三层楼阁式砖塔，塔高 7 米左右，底边长 2 米。

　　玄奘墓塔塔刹下为刹座，上为覆钵、莲瓣、宝瓶和宝珠等。

　　1978 年对墓塔进行过大规模维修，在墓塔基座中发现唐代佛教文物 600 多件。其中有大量佛像和写经。内有一尊金质观音像，重 1135 克，高 24 厘米，极为珍贵。

Located in Xingjiao Temple of Chang'an district, the southern suburbs of Xi'an, Xuanzang Tomb Pagoda was built in 669 during Tang dynasty. Buddhist master Xuanzang died in 664 in Yuhua Palace, Junxian county of Shaanxi province. According to his will, he was buried in White Deer Plain near Xi'an, a

玄奘法师墓塔和窥基、圆测二弟子灵塔（朱静玥摄影）

remote and quite place far from the imperial palace. Xuanzang's sacred relics were transferred to Xingjiao Temple in 669 and a pagoda was built then.

Xuanzang was born with the name of "Chen Yi" around 602 in Goushi town, Luoyang city, Henan province.

In the rest of his life, he committed himself to translating the sutras he brought back from India and he also translated one of the Chinese classics *Laozi* into Sanskrit to be introduced into India. *Traveling Records of the Western Regions in Great Tang Dynasty*, which was written by other people according to Xuanzang's dictation, is an important book to study ancient history and geography of India, Nepal, Pakistan and Bangladesh and other countries in middle Asia.

Facing south, the square five-storey brick pagoda is 23 meters high and each side of the ground storey is 5.2 meters long. Inside the niche on the south side of the ground storey is a clay statue of Xuanzang, while a stone inscription titled *Inscription in Honor of Master Tang Sanzang* also known as the *Dabianjue Master*, is on the northern wall. From the second storey and above, the pagoda is solid and people cannot climb upstairs.

The bottom part of the spire is the spire base, on which there are inverted bowl, lotus petals, precious bottle and precious bead. The small pagoda on the east side is built for Xuanzang's senior disciple, Yuance, and on the west side stands the other one for his another senior disciple, Kuiji. The two small brick pagodas are both three-storey and in pavilion-style. They are about 7 meters high and each side of the ground storey is 2 meters long.

A large scale of repair was made in 1978, and more than 600 pieces of Buddhist relics of Tang dynasty were found, including many statues of Buddha and Buddhism scriptures, among which there is a very precious gold statue of Bodhisattva that weighs 1135 grams and is 24 centimeters high.

陕西西安大雁塔

Big Wild Goose Pagoda Shaanxi Province

西安大雁塔邮票（中国 1994 年发行）

西安大雁塔位于西安市大慈恩寺西院。建于唐高宗永徽三年（公元 652 年）。现塔高 64.7 米，是一座楼阁式方形七层空心砖塔。

在玄奘主持慈恩寺期间，以"恐人代不常，经本散失兼防火难"为由，希望妥善安置经像舍利，拟在慈恩寺正门外造石塔一座，于唐高宗永徽三年（公元 652 年）三月附图表上奏。恩准由朝廷资助在慈恩寺西院建五层砖塔。由玄奘亲自主持建造，历时两年建成。此塔砖面土心，不能登临，每层皆存舍利。

大雁塔以后曾多次改扩建。武则天长安年间（公元 701—704 年）武则天与王公贵族捐资，在塔的原址上重建为七层仿木结构楼阁式砖塔。再后在明万历三十二年（公元 1604 年）进行了一次重大维修加固，在原塔外完整地砌上了 60 厘米厚的砖包层，使大雁塔成为现塔模样。

大雁塔总高 64.7 米，塔基东西长 45.7 米，南北长 48 米。塔身以磨砖对缝砌筑，塔内各层有楼板，木梯达塔顶。

大雁塔塔身底层南门的门楣和门框上有线刻精美佛像和砖雕对联。南门内廊道两侧布满雁塔题字石刻。

这门洞两侧还有玄奘法师的两通碑刻，东侧是"玄奘负笈图"碑，西侧是"玄奘译经图"碑。

南门外两侧碑龛内有两通唐代石碑，西侧是《大唐三藏圣教之序》碑，东侧是《大唐三藏圣教序记》碑。

《大唐三藏圣教之序》碑由唐太宗李世民撰文，褚遂良手书。

《大唐三藏圣教序记》碑由唐高宗李治撰文，褚遂良手书。这两通唐代碑刻高 337.5 厘米，下宽 100 厘米。

值得注意的是，这两通石碑字体都是竖排，但竖排文字的左右排列方式不同。《大唐三藏圣教之序》碑是自右向左排，而《大唐三藏圣教序记》碑则是自左向右排列。

大雁塔的二层塔室内供奉铜质鎏金佛祖像。

三层供有佛舍利和大雁塔模型。此舍利是一位印度友人所赠，其中一颗骨舍利，直径 3.5 毫米，一颗血舍利，直径 1.5 毫米。

塔身四层供奉着两片贝叶经。

塔身五层陈列一通"佛祖足迹碑"，足迹上有诸多佛教图案，内涵十分丰富，素有"见足如见佛，拜足如拜佛"之说。

塔身六层悬有唐代五位诗人的诗作。

塔身七层塔顶刻有莲花藻井，中央是硕大莲花，花瓣上写有 14 字连环诗，因无标点，顺时针阅读，可有多种读法。这 14 字是"前人赞唐僧取经还须游西天拜佛"。

关于大雁塔塔名的由来，有几种说法，较为可信的是如下说法。相传很久以前，古印度的一所寺院，信奉小乘佛教，吃三净食，即"雁、鹿、犊肉"。一天，空中飞来一群大雁，有一和尚信口说，"今天大家都没东西吃了，菩萨应知道我们肚子饿呀"，话音未落，一只雁坠死在他面前，他惊喜交加，通告众僧，都认为是如来佛祖在教化他们，于是在雁落之处葬雁建塔，塔名即为"雁塔"。后来，玄奘游学印度时，瞻仰了这座雁塔，回国后，在慈恩寺建一砖塔，即命名大雁塔。此说法在《大唐西域记》中有记载。

大雁塔塔刹高 4.87 米，刹座为覆钵体，上有葫芦状宝珠，其上是一大宝珠（或称三重葫芦状宝刹）。

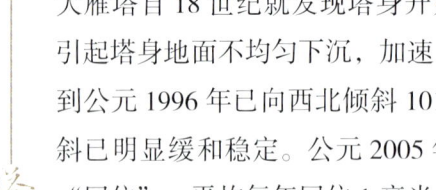

大雁塔自 18 世纪就发现塔身开始倾斜。20 世纪中叶，因地下水位下降，引起塔身地面不均匀下沉，加速了塔身倾斜。公元1985年已倾斜998毫米，到公元 1996 年已向西北倾斜 1010.5 毫米。经过 20 多年综合治理，雁塔倾斜已明显缓和稳定。公元 2005 年倾斜量已回到 1001.9 毫米，雁塔已开始"回位"，平均每年回位 1 毫米。

Located in Daci'en Temple south of the historical city of Xi'an, the Big Wild Goose Pagoda was built in 652 during the reign of Emperor Gaozong of Tang dynasty. The square seven-storey brick pagoda is 64.7 meters high and is in pavilion style.

When Master Xuanzang was the head of Daci'en Temple, he made a proposal to the royal court to build a stone pagoda to preserve the scriptures outside the temple for the reason that the unpredictable affairs and difficulty in fireproofing might lead to the damage and loss of the scriptures. He also offered a blueprint imitating the structure of pagodas he saw in India. Having got permission from

玄奘法师塑像（朱静玥摄影）

Emperor Gaozong, Xuanzang supervised the construction of the pagoda inside the temple. It took two years to complete the construction. The pagoda was originally a five-storey brick structure made of muds and bricks, and could not be accessible. Buddhist relics were kept on each storey.

Big Wild Goose Pagoda later experienced many times of reconstruction and extension. With the donations of the Empress and nobles, the building was renovated into a seven-storey pavilion-style brick structure during the reign of Empress Wu Zetian. The outer walls of the pagoda were covered by a thick layer of bricks in Ming dynasty as it is today.

The Big Wild Goose Pagoda, as we see today, is 64.7 meters high, 48 meters in length from north to south, and 45.7 meters from east to west. It is built with layers of bricks, without any cement in between. Inside the pagoda, there are wooden stairs winding to the top.

The door-frames of the south gate of the ground storey are caved with delicate statues of Buddha and couplet, and the interior walls of the gateway are inlaid with carvings of inscriptions. Among them are the picture of Xuanzang carrying a box of Buddhist scriptures and the picture of Xuanzang translating Buddhist scriptures on the east and west side respectively.

On either side of the exterior walls of the south gate stand two large stone tablets, which are 337.5 centimeters in height and 100 centimeters in width downside. On the west side is the tablet of *Preface to Xuanzang's Translation of the Buddhist Scriptures* by Emperor Tang Taizong carved in Chu Suiliang's calligraphy and on the other side is the tablet of *Preface to Xuanzang's Translation of the Buddhist Scriptures* by Emperor Tang Gaozong carved in Chu Suiliang's handwriting.

It is worth noting that the characters of the inscriptions on two tablets are both written in vertical columns but arranged in different ways. The words of *Preface to Xuanzang's Translation of the Buddhist Scriptures* have to be read from right to left, while the words of the other inscription have to be read from left to right.

Inside the niche of the second storey is enshrined a gilt bronze Buddha *figurine* of Ming dynasty. On the center of the third storey, a wooden seat with

西安大雁塔（朱静玥摄影）

Buddhist relics and the model of Big Goose Pagoda is displayed. The relics were given as presents by an Indian Master. The diameters of the two Buddhist relics are 3.5 millimeters and 1.5 millimeters respectively. On the fourth storey, there are two pieces of Pattra-leaf scriptures (replicas). There displays, on the fifth storey, the Buddha footprint tablet with many designs of Buddhism and, on the sixth storey, the poems of five poets of Tang dynasty.

A caisson ceiling of lotus is carved on the seventh storey, with a huge lotus in the center and lotus petals carved with a poem of fourteen characters. Since there is no punctuation, the poem can have different meanings when it is read clockwise.

As for the reason why it is called Big Wild Goose Pagoda, there are several old stories. According to a famous Buddhist parable, there was a temple of Hinayana in ancient India. As Hinayana believers, the monks there could eat the food within the "three prohibitions", namely the meat from wild goose, deer and veal that's not killed, seen and smelt by them. One day, seeing a group of big wild geese flying by, a monk said to himself, "Today we have no meat to eat. I hope the merciful Bodhisattva knows we are hungry and will give us some." At that very moment, the leading wild goose crushed to the earth and died right before him. All the monks were startled and believed that Buddha showed his spirit to order them to be more pious. They buried the goose and erected a pagoda named Wild Goose Pagoda. Afterwards, Xuanzang visited the pagoda when he was in India. After he came back, he built a similar pagoda in Ci'en Temple named Big Wild Goose Pagoda. The story was recorded in *Traveling Records of the Western Regions in Great Tang Dynasty*.

The spire of the pagoda is 4.87 meters high, and its base is in the shape of inverted bowl. There is a cucurbit-shaped bead topped with another huge bead.

Because of repeated man-made sabotage coupled with its structural problems, the Big Wild Goose Pagoda was discovered to incline since the 18th century. In the 1960s, as a result of the surrounding excessive exploitation of groundwater, the water pressure dropped significantly, causing a wide range of uneven ground subsidence, accelerating the sink of the pagoda. After more than 20 years' comprehensive renovation, the situation of Big Wild Goose Pagoda has become stable.

甘肃崆峒山凌空塔

Lingkong Pagoda Gansu Province

崆峒山凌空塔邮票（中国 2003 年发行）

　　崆峒山凌空塔位于甘肃省崆峒山中台。崆峒山是儒释道并存的圣地，道教兴盛，也有不少佛教寺庙。凌空塔（也叫凌云塔）原在舒花寺内，佛寺已不存，只有佛塔尚在。凌空塔始建于北宋天圣年间，明万历十三年（公元 1585 年）曾维修并留有题记。

　　凌空塔高约 30 米，底面宽 10.5 米，是一座七级八面楼阁式砖塔，塔内原有木梯可达塔顶。底层南面开券门，二层以上正面辟券门，门的两侧辟小窗或佛龛，门内、窗内及佛龛内皆供佛像。

　　凌空塔塔顶还长着大小两棵松树，称为"塔托双松"。佛塔虽经维修，但双松仍旧保留了下来。

　　凌空塔塔身略向西倾斜，凌空塔塔顶收成覆斗形，上置塔刹。塔刹以铁铸造，分三层，下为大宝珠，上为葫芦状双宝珠。中部有 30 字铭文，"大明国承宣布政平凉府崆峒山镇宝塔鼎一坐 万历十四年五月五日吉造"，证明万历十四年（公元 1586 年）曾对凌空塔进行过维修。

Lingkong Pagoda is located on Kongtong Mountain, Gansu province. Kongtong Mountain is a holy place for Taoism, but there are still some Buddhist temples built here. Lingkong Pagoda, also known as Lingyun Pagoda, was originally built inside Shuhua Temple that had been destroyed. The pagoda was first constructed during Tiansheng period of North Song dynasty, and was repaired in the thirteenth year of Wanli period of Ming dynasty. An inscription was left recording this maintenance.

Lingkong Pagoda is about 30 meters high and is 10.5 meters wide at the bottom. The octahedral pagoda is a seven-storey pavilion-style building, and there is a wooden staircase inside leading to the top of pagoda. There is a door on the south side of the ground storey, and a door on the right side of second storey and up, on either side of which there are small windows or niches with statues of Buddha inside.

崆峒山凌空塔附近（秦槐键摄影）

Two pine trees grow on top of the pagoda. Although some repairing works were made to the pagoda, the trees survive.

The pagoda inclines slightly to the west, and its top is shaped like inverted dipper with a spire on it. The spire is made of iron and has three layers. A huge precious bead is at the bottom, topped with two cucurbit-shaped beads. There is an inscription of 30 words, in the middle part of the steeple, which says the pagoda used to be repaired in the fourteenth year of Wanli period of Ming dynasty.

崆峒山凌空塔（秦槐键摄影）

江苏镇江慈寿塔

Cishou Pagoda Jiangsu Province

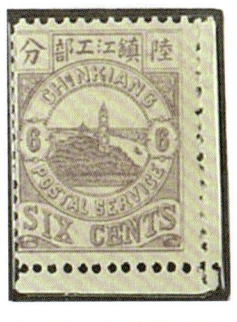

（第一版 1894年镇江书信馆发行）
镇江慈寿塔邮票

（第二版 1895年镇江书信馆发行）
镇江慈寿塔邮票

　　镇江慈寿塔位于江苏镇江金山上。慈寿塔始建于南北朝齐梁时期，现塔是清末重建的。慈寿塔为砖木结构楼阁式塔，八角七级。砖砌塔身，木构外檐，内有木梯可认塔顶。

　　慈寿塔修建的原因，据说是北宋丞相曾布为超度亡母在金山上建南北双塔，皇帝赐名"荐寿塔"和"荐慈塔"，明初俱废。

　　清咸丰年间该塔毁于战火，到清光绪年间，金山寺住持隐儒募捐集资，他沿门托钵，约历五年，到光绪二十六年（公元1901年），塔建成。

　　慈寿塔在咸丰年间被毁，实际上是塔的木构部分和塔刹被焚，但砖砌塔身仍在。在镇江书信馆1894年发行的邮票和清末香港发行的明信片上，慈寿塔就是这样。

　　慈寿塔的塔刹十分华丽，底部是刹座，上面是纺锤状七层相轮和宝盖。再上是露盘和宝葫芦状刹顶。宝盖上悬八只风铃，另系八条长链，长链下端系于塔顶八只檐角上。

Located on Jinshan Hill, Zhenjiang city, Jiangsu province, Cishou Pagoda was built during Qiliang Period of Northern and Southern dynasties. The present structure of the pagoda was rebuilt at the end of Qing dynasty. With its main body made of brick, and with its eaves, balconies and balustrades made of wood, the pagoda is an octagonal seven-storey building. Each storey has doors facing in four directions and spiral staircases inside.

Cishou Pagoda was allegedly constructed by Zeng Bu, the prime minister of Northern Song dynasty. Zeng Bu built two pagodas, named Jianshou Pagoda and Jianci Pagoda by the Emperor, on north and south part of Jinshan Hill in honor of his mother. At the early stage of Ming dynasty, the pagodas were abandoned.

Cishou Pagoda were damaged because of war during the reign of Xianfeng Emperor of Qing dynasty, and during the reign of Guangxu Emperor, another new pagoda was built by Yinru, the head of Jinshan Temple, who had gone around collecting money for five years for the construction of the pagoda.

The wooden parts and the steeple of the pagoda were damaged during the reign of Xianfeng Emperor of Qing dynasty, but the pagoda body made of bricks

镇江慈寿塔附近（燕峘宇摄影）

镇江慈寿塔（燕岨宇摄影）

survived. Featured in the stamp issued in 1894 and the postage card issued in Hong Kong, the pagoda looked as what it was at the time.

The spire of Cishou Pagoda looks magnificent and is composed of a base, spindle-shaped discs, the canopy, the dew plate, and the cucurbit-shaped top. Eight wind bells hang at the angles of the canopy which are connected with eight eaves of the pagoda top by eight long chains.

江苏苏州虎丘塔

Tiger Hill Pagoda Jiangsu Province

苏州虎丘塔邮票（中国 1983 年发行）

苏州虎丘塔位于苏州城外虎丘山上，又名云岩寺塔。佛塔始建于隋仁寿元年（公元 601 年），始为木塔，后毁，于公元 961 年建成砖塔。佛塔为八面七层楼阁式，砖木结构，砖砌塔身，木构外檐，塔高 47.7 米。

虎丘塔是一座斜塔。自塔建成以来屡毁屡修。由于地基原因，从明代起开始倾斜，越来越严重，经测量，现在佛塔向西北倾斜，塔顶偏离中心 2.34 米，倾斜 3 度 59 分。

虎丘塔倾斜的原因，是由于佛塔是建在山坡上，山坡西南高、东北低。塔下的土层厚薄不一，且是一种人工填埋的杂土，以致地基渗水、潜流冲刷，地基中的杂土颗粒流失，产生空隙，故而造成不均匀下沉，塔体倾斜。

公元 1949 年以后，虎丘塔已是严重破败、千疮百孔，处于即将坍塌的状态。为了保护虎丘塔，迄今进行了三次维修。第一次维修是在公元 1956—1957 年，主要是加固塔身，即在每层塔身外加三道铁箍，外抹水泥，使塔转危为安。这次加固塔身，挽救了塔身，但加重了塔体重量，从而也加剧了塔的倾斜。

苏州虎丘塔（燕岠宇摄影）

第二次维修是在公元 1978—1980 年，主要是加固地基。浇灌混凝土将地基和地坪连成一体。

公元 1956 年维修塔时，在第三层的夹层中发现石函、经箱、铜佛、铜镜和越窑青瓷莲花碗等珍贵文物。

虎丘塔在第二次大修后，经过 20 多年，又发生了新问题。一是雨雪侵蚀，塔身存在冻蚀现象，砖块崩坏脱落，塔身出现裂缝，甚至生出小树。再是塔体木构件开始腐烂、虫蛀。所以从公元 2014 年开始第三次整修。

Located on Tiger Hill, Suzhou city, Jiangsu province, Tiger Hill Pagoda, also known as Yunyan Temple Pagoda, was first constructed in 601, Sui dynasty. Later the wooden structure was damaged and a new brick pagoda was built in 961. The octahedral seven-storey pagoda is brick and wood structure with a total height of 47.7 meters.

Tiger Hill Pagoda has the distinction of being China's Leaning Tower. It is said that the pagoda has been leaning since Ming dynasty, and things has got even worse afterwards for the reason of its foundation problems. It is measured that the pagoda has leant 3.59 degrees to the northwest and its top and bottom vary by 2.34 meters.

The pagoda is leaning because it is built on a sloping hill, southwest side higher than the other side. Besides, the soil layer underground varies in thickness, and half of it is rock, the other half is on soil. As a result, the foundations have subsided unevenly causing the inclination of the pagoda.

In 1956, efforts were made to stabilize the pagoda. Three lines of hoop iron were added to fasten the pagoda's body, and the outer walls were covered with a layer of cement. While the pagoda was reinforced after the repair, its body weighs heavier, resulting in even further leaning.

The second repair was made between 1978 and 1980 to consolidate the pagoda and prevent slant from becoming more serious. Concrete piles have been driven into the ground around the pagoda in order to reinforce the foundation.

During the reinforcement process in 1956, some Buddhist treasures have been found, such as a stone casket containing Buddhist scriptures, bronze statue of Buddha, bronze mirror and Yue kiln porcelains.

New problems arose twenty years after the second repair. One was that cracks appeared because of the erosion by rain and snow. Some bricks fell off from the body of the pagoda and small trees grew from the cracks. The other problem was that the wooden components had been decaying and damaged by worms. Therefore, another repair was made in 2014.

浙江杭州雷峰塔

Leifeng Pagoda Zhejiang Province

杭州雷峰塔邮票（加纳 2001 年发行）

　　雷峰塔位于杭州西湖南岸夕照山的雷峰之上。该塔始建于南北朝时期，新塔建于 2002 年。现塔高 71.67 米，为八面五层楼阁式，砖木混合结构，是现代工艺建造的佛塔。

　　雷峰塔是五代十国时期吴越国王钱俶为奉藏佛祖螺髻发舍利而建，又传说是他为祝贺其妃生子而建，故此塔又称黄妃塔。明代嘉靖年间（公元 1555 年）倭寇将塔焚毁，之后修复。雷峰塔在公元 1924 年倾塌，究其原因，一是自然风雨侵蚀，再是人为破坏。当时有人迷信，认为塔砖有镇邪和治病的功效，不时有人偷挖塔砖，久而久之，导致佛塔倒塌。

　　雷峰塔于公元 2002 年重建竣工。按旧塔形制八面五层楼阁式，分为三部分，塔基、塔身和塔刹。自上而下分别是塔刹、五层、四层、三层、二层、暗层、底层、基台上层、基台底层。新塔轴心与旧塔相同。基台坚固宽大，实际上是罩在整个旧塔遗址之上，以保护旧塔遗址。塔内设楼梯，塔中心建电梯，直达塔顶。

　　旧塔遗址上围以玻璃，从基台上层可俯瞰遗址全貌，有人还给遗址舍钱币。佛塔每层的出檐上覆以铜瓦，各角悬风铎。

塔顶为塔刹，刹座是两层多角素面柱，上为七层纺锤形相轮和宝盖。刹顶为圆光、仰月和多连宝珠。

雷峰塔新塔兴建清理塔基时，发现地宫。地宫面积不大，长宽各 0.5 米，深约 1 米。地宫中出土青铜佛像和铁函，铁函内藏阿育王塔等 60 余件珍贵文物。

阿育王塔高 35 厘米，边长 12.6 厘米。塔的四面饰有佛祖故事题材的浅浮雕，塔内有金瓶，其内藏佛祖螺髻发舍利。佛祖螺髻发舍利的发现，轰动了世界佛教界。

雷峰塔在公元 1924 年倒塌时，原藏在塔顶的藏经砖散落一地。藏经砖内藏有古代木版印刷的《宝箧印陀罗尼经》。

在古代，人们通常把佛经的一段卷在一竹签上，外裹黄绢，塞入特制的砖孔内，再塞木栓封口，是为藏经砖。

Located on Xizhao Peak, the southeast side of the Hangzhou West Lake, Leifeng Pagoda was originally built during Northern and Southern dynasties and rebuilt in 2002. The residual octagonal brick pagoda is 71.67 meters tall, and is in pavilion style with five storeys.

Leifeng Pagoda was constructed during Five Dynasties and Ten Kingdoms by the king of Wuyue Kingdom to house the hair and skeletal remains of Sakyamuni, the founder of Buddhism. The pagoda is also said to be built by the king to celebrate the pregnancy of his favorite concubine, Huangfei. Thus, it was originally named Huangfei Pagoda.

However, during the reign of Jiajing Emperor of Ming dynasty, the pagoda was burnt down by illegally-entering Japanese bandits, called "Wokou" at the time. Afterwards the pagoda was renovated. Leifeng Pagoda collapsed in 1924 for the reason of erosion by wind and rain and the damages made by humans. Due to a superstition that the bricks from the pagoda could repel illness or suppress the evils, many people stole bricks from the pagoda to grind into powder. Finally, the pagoda collapsed as a result of disrepair in 1924.

The newly-built Leifeng Pagoda opened in 2002. It was constructed on the former site and preserved its traditional pavilion style. The octahedral five-storey pagoda is composed of three major parts: the base, the body and the steeple. The structure consists of, from top to bottom, the steeple, the fifth storey, the

杭州雷峰塔（王乃强摄影）

fourth, the third, the second, the hidden storey, the ground storey and the base. There is a staircase and elevator leading to the top of the pagoda.

The site of the former pagoda is enclosed with glass. Standing on the platform, people can have an overall view of the site of the original tower through glass. Some people throw coins into the site as a way of prayer and Benediction. The eaves of each storey are covered with bronze tiles, and wind bells hang at every angle of the eaves.

On the pagoda top is the spire comprised of a two-layer precious casket, the discs, the canopy, the circular polarization, the crescent moon, and the precious bead.

The underground palace was excavated when the foundation was reconditioned in the process of the construction of the new pagoda. The underground palace is not very large, half a meter long and wide, about 1 meter deep. Over 60 pieces of precious relics, such as gilded bronze statues of Buddha and the emperor Asoka tower, are unearthed. The emperor Asoka tower, 35 centimeters tall, 12.6 centimeters in the length of the side, is decorated on four sides with bas-relief carvings featured in stories of Buddha. There is a gold case inside the tower containing the hair and skeletal remains of Sakyamuni. The discovery of the Buddhist relics is a sensation in the circle of Buddhism worldwide.

Found inside the bricks falling off the pagoda top when the building collapsed in 1924 was a blocked printed Buddhist scripture Karandavyuha Dharani Sutra. In ancient time, people rolled a piece of Buddhist text around a bamboo stick, wrapped it with yellow silk and inserted it into the specially-made holes in the bricks and sealed the holes with corks.

浙江杭州六和塔

Pagoda of Six Harmonies Zhejiang Province

杭州六和塔邮票（中国 1994 年发行）

　　杭州六和塔位于杭州钱塘江畔的月轮山上。始建于北宋开宝三年（公元 970 年），是僧人智元禅师为镇江潮而建。

　　塔为八面十三层楼阁式砖木结构，塔高 59.89 米，占地 888 平方米，外形雍容大度，气宇不凡。

　　六和塔和其他古塔一样，屡毁屡建，屡毁屡修。北宋宣和三年（公元 1121 年）毁于兵祸，塔和寺都片瓦不存，至公元 1163 年重建。明嘉靖年间（公元 1533 年）遭倭寇火焚，只余砖砌塔身。

　　六和塔于明万历年间重修。清咸丰年间又遭火焚，至清光绪年间大修，此次大修使六和塔的结构基本定形。

　　公元 1949 年后又有几次修缮，最重要的是公元 1986—1991 年，调整了屋面坡度，更换了全部屋瓦。

　　六和塔内结构复杂，塔身十三层中有六层是封闭的，另七层与塔身内部相通，七明六暗，塔内只有七层回廊。

　　从六和塔的水平剖面看，从外往里可分外墙、回廊、内墙和塔心室。

六和塔的内墙也有门通往塔心室，塔心室有佛龛。

两层回廊之间有楼梯相通。木檐之下有外廊，人们可从回廊通向木檐外廊，从外廊可眺览塔外风光。六和塔的塔壁上雕刻着人物花卉、鸟兽鱼虫等各式花纹图案，栩栩如生。

塔刹的结构简单，下为基座，上为大宝珠、仰莲和宝珠。

Located on Yuelun Mountain besides Qiantang River in Hangzhou City, Zhejiang Province, the pagoda was first constructed in 970 during Northern Song dynasty by a Buddhist monk Zhiyuan. At that time, the pagoda was built to suppress the tidewater. The pagoda is an octagonal building with a height of 59.89 meters and covers an area of 888 square meters. It is made of wood and brick and is in pavilion style. Seen from the outside, the 13-storey pagoda looks beautiful and magnificent.

Just as many other pagodas, Six Harmonies Pagoda has undergone some destructions and repairs. During the reign of the Xuanhe Emperor, the Pagoda and the temple were completely destroyed by a war. The pagoda was rebuilt in 1156 during the reign of Jiajing Emperor of Ming dynasty and was burnt down by Japanese invaders. Only the brick body survived and was repaired during the reign of Wanli Emperor of Ming dynasty. The newly built pagoda was again damaged by a fire during the reign of Xianfeng Emperor of Qing dynasty and extensive repairs were made during Guangxu reign of Qing dynasty. The major repairs made after the founding of the nation were mainly on the roof, the slope reconditioned, the tiles completely replaced.

The structure of the pagoda is sophisticated. Among its thirteen storeys, six of them are enclosed, while the other seven storeys are open inside and have zigzagged corridors. Seen from the horizontal cross section, from outside to inside, the pagoda is divided into four parts: the outer wall, the cloister, the inner wall and a small room, forming two rings.

Doors are opened on interior walls, with the passageway leading to the small room at the heart. In the room there are niches enshrined with statues of Buddha.

杭州六和塔（王乃强摄影）

Between two rings is the corridor, and the stairs are available in the corridor. A leaning pole is fixed at the corner of outer wall, connected with the wood eaves. From the outer corridors, people can have a good view of the Qiantang River meandering far into the distance.

The walls are decorated with brick carvings, which feature a wide range of motifs, including figures, flowers, birds, beasts and fish and so on. These brick carvings are rare material proofs of Chinese ancient architectures.

The spire of the pagoda is simple in structure, which consists of a base and a huge precious bead, blooming lotus and a small bead on the top.

福建泉州镇国塔

Zhenguo Pagoda Fujian Province

泉州镇国塔邮票（加纳 1996 年发行）

　　镇国塔位于泉州开元寺大雄宝殿前面东侧，始建于唐咸通六年（公元 865 年），塔高 48.24 米，现塔为八角五层楼阁式石塔。

　　镇国塔的建造历程富有戏剧性。唐咸通六年（公元 865 年）由文僳禅师主持建造，始为木塔。宋天禧年间（公元 1017—1021 年）改为十三层木塔，绍兴年间（公元 1155 年）遭火焚。

　　宋宝庆三年（公元 1227 年）改建为七层砖塔。宋嘉熙二年（公元 1238 年）僧人本洪改建为石塔，但他只建了一层，僧人法权续建到四层，天竺讲僧天锡续建了第五层。

　　镇国塔用花岗岩建造。

　　镇国塔塔身有 80 幅浮雕，刻有 80 尊人物。

　　五层塔分为五乘，按佛教等级由低到高，表明修行的五种境界。第一层雕四大天王、天后八部和四大金刚等；第二层雕阿罗汉；第三层雕尊者罗汉；第四层雕观世音、文殊、普贤和地藏王菩萨等，第四层还有梁武帝的雕像；第五层雕的是释迦牟尼、药师玻璃光佛、阿弥陀佛和弥勒佛。

泉州镇国塔（邑石网供图）

镇国塔须弥座上则有佛教故事雕刻。

镇国塔塔刹高 11.1 米，底部为刹座，上面是宝瓶，再上是七层相轮、宝盖、水烟、葫芦状双宝珠。宝盖处用八条铁链，系于顶层檐角。

Located east in front of the main Hall of Kaiyuan Temple，Quanzhou city，Zhenguo Pagoda was first built in the year 865 during the reign of Xiantong Emperor of Tang dynasty. The pavilion-style stone pagoda is 48.24 meters high，and has five storeys.

The construction and reconstruction of Zhenguo Pagoda took quite a long time and many changes had been made in this process. The pagoda was built in the year 865 during Xiantong reign of Tang dynasty，supervised by a Buddhist monk Wen Cheng. The pagoda was originally wood structure and was reconstructed into a 13-storey building during Tianxi reign of Song dynasty. It was burnt down in the year 1155 during Shaoxing reign of Southern Song dynasty.

In the year 1227 of Song dynasty the pagoda was restored into a seven-storey brick building. Another Buddhist monk Benhong changed it into a stone structure in 1238 of Southern Song dynasty. But all he had finished was the construction of the first storey and the other four storeys were built by monk Faquan and Indian monk Tianxi. The stone material selected for the construction was granite.

The pagoda body was decorated with 80 figure carvings. It is divided into five layers according to the ranks of Buddhism，indicating five realms of Buddhist practice. The first layer is carved with Four Heavenly Kings，the Queens of heaven，Four Heavenly Guardians，the second layer arhats，the third layer master arhat，the fourth layer Avalokitesvara，Manjusri，Samantabhadr and statue of the first emperor of Liang Kingdom，Wudi，the fifth layer Shakyamuni Buddha，Amitabha and Maitreya. The Sumeru pedestal is decorated with carvings of Buddhist stories.

The spire of the pagoda is 11.1 meters high. On its base are precious bottle，the discs，the canopy，the water smoke and the cucurbit-shaped beads. The canopy is connected with the eaves of the top storey by eight iron chains.

重庆报恩塔
Baoen Pagoda Chongqing

重庆报恩塔邮票

（第一版 1893 年重庆书信馆发行）

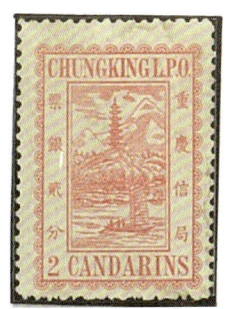

重庆报恩塔邮票

（第三版 1894 年重庆书信馆发行）

重庆报恩塔位于重庆市长江东岸的莲花山觉林寺，建于清乾隆二十二年（公元 1757 年），是座八角九层楼阁式砖石塔。塔高 45 米，塔基周长 46 米。各层有门及小窗，塔内有石梯可直达塔顶。报恩塔一至七层的中心室辟有佛龛，供奉佛像。

报恩塔所在的觉林寺早已不存，只余地名，报恩塔所在公交车站就叫觉林寺站。

报恩塔相传是一位名为月江的和尚建造的。月江和尚在莲花山觉林寺出家，他的祖母死后就葬在莲花山，他为尽孝，就在觉林寺修造佛塔，塔名为"报恩塔"。

但报恩塔尚未完工，月江和尚就圆寂了。之后他的弟子善明继续修建此塔，终于在公元 1773 年完成。

关于重庆报恩塔的名字，在报恩塔的塔院门楣上刻着"报恩塔"三个大字。在两侧门框上，还刻着一副对联，分别是"因传心经分三教"和"为建浮屠报四恩"。

塔刹构造特殊，在一个八角形覆钵状基座上，设三个串在一起的铁质圆球，相当于三层相轮。其上有仰莲，再上是宝珠。

关于重庆报恩塔的层数，实际上是九层，但有人说是七层。世界第一套佛塔邮票上画的也是七层，有人说是七层，系误传。

重庆报恩塔正门（燕峒宇摄影）

重庆报恩塔（燕岖宇摄影）

Located in the Juelin Temple on the Lianhua Mountain of Chongqing city, the pagoda was first constructed in 1757 during the reign of Qianlong Emperor, Qing dynasty. The pagoda is an octagonal building with a height of 45 meters and the perimeter of the base is 46 meters. Seen from the outside, the brick and stone pagoda has 9 storeys and is in pavilion style. There are doors and small windows on each storey and stone stairs leading to the pagoda top. The central room of the first seven storeys has niches enshrined with statues of Buddha.

Juelin Temple where the pagoda is situated is no longer in existence, but the name of the temple has been handed down. The bus stop of the place is named "Juelinsi".

Bao'en Pagoda is said to be constructed by a monk Yuejiang who became a Buddhist monk at Juelin Temple of Lianhua Mountain. His grandmother was buried, after her death, in the mountain and therefore he built a pagoda to fulfill his filial duty to her. The pagoda was thus named Bao'en, meaning expressing gratitude.

Unfortunately, the monk died before the construction was completed. Shanming, one of his disciples, continued the work and finished the project in 1773.

The pagoda got its present name Bao'en, literally meaning "doing favors in return", because these words are carved in the door-head of the building. On both sides of the door frame are carved with couplets describing the purpose of construction of the pagoda.

The structure of the spire is quite different from others. On the octagonal base shaped as inverted bowl are three iron balls strung together, blooming lotus and a precious bead.

There is no agreement as to the numbers of the storeys of the pagoda. Some people believe that the pagoda has seven storeys, for the building first featured in the stamps worldwide is seven-storey.

However, there are actually nine storeys in the pagoda. What appears in the stamp is only a part of the structure. Therefore it is mistaken that the pagoda has seven storeys.

云南大理千寻塔

Qianxun Pagoda Yunnan Province

大理千寻塔邮票（中国 1958 年发行）

　　大理千寻塔位于大理市西北，东临洱海，西对苍山。塔高 69.13 米，塔身方形，是十六重密檐式砖塔。

　　千寻塔始建于南诏保和年间（公元 824—859 年）。塔东临洱海，时有水患，有记载"错金为顶，顶有金鹏，世传龙性敬塔而畏鹏，大理旧为龙泽，故以此镇之"。可见此塔是为镇龙而建。

　　大理千寻塔塔身四壁厚 3.3 米，第 2 至 15 层每层正中交错辟佛龛，龛内供佛像。顶层为实心。

　　塔底层东面开门，西开一窗。塔身中部微凸，上部收分缓和，塔状如梭，端庄素雅。

　　千寻塔塔刹底层为覆钵刹座。覆钵直径 2.28 米，覆钵以上有仰莲、相轮、双圈宝盖及葫芦状双宝珠。

　　千寻塔在公元 1977 年在维修时，在塔顶和塔基出土了大批文物。在塔顶出土各种人物造像、佛塔模型、青铜镜、各种药物、各种法器，还有写经，但多已腐烂。

塔基出土百余件陶制佛像和陶制塔模。

千寻塔的文物中最可贵的是一尊高 24 厘米的纯金观音像。从其面貌、发式和衣着看是一位女性，但其上身裸露，却是男身。观音像在唐代以前都是男性，以后逐渐本土化、世俗化，观音像逐渐变为女性。有宋一代，世俗化较为显著。据查，这批人物像是大理国时代（12 世纪）铸造和入藏的，这相当于是在南宋时代。这尊观音像可以认为是一种过渡时期的产物，所以其意义十分重大。

Located northwest of scenic Dali, Yunnan province, The square Qianxun Pagoda is 69.13 meters high and has thirteen layer of eaves.

Qianxun Pagoda, facing Erhai Lake to the west, was first built during the

大理三塔－千寻塔居中(邑石网供图)

reign of Baohe of Nanzhao Kingdom. Because floods often struck the area at that time, the pagoda was constructed in order to repel the disaster.

The walls of the four sides of the pagoda body are 3.3 meters in thickness. There are niches in the storeys except the ground storey and the top storey, which are solid inside.

Doors are open on the east and west sides of the ground storey. There is also a window on the west side. The middle part of the pagoda is a little wider than the other parts, and the upper part tapers slightly, which makes the pagoda shaped like a shuttle.

The base of the pagoda spire is in the shape of inverted bowl, with the diameter of 2.28 meters. On the inverted bowl are blooming lotus, the discs, and the canopy, topped with two cucurbit-shaped beads.

A lot of treasures were excavated from the base and the top of the pagoda when it was being renovated in 1997. Unearthed from the pagoda top were various statues of figure, model of Buddhist pagoda, bronze mirror, medicines, ritual instruments and some scriptures which had mostly been rotten. From the foundation were unearthed millions of clay statues of Buddha and clay models of Buddhist pagoda.

云南盈江永燕塔

Yongyan Pagoda Yunnan Province

盈江永燕塔邮票（中国 1998 年发行）

　　盈江永（允）燕塔位于盈江县城以东的允燕山上。1947 年由盈江盏达土司思洪升为镇水妖募资建造，由于战争瘟疫等原因，到 1955 年才建成。

　　整个塔群由一座主塔和 40 座小塔组成。主塔高 20 米。塔的基座为方形，共有五层，由下而上逐层收缩。第一层每面立七座小塔，第二层开始只在每层角上立一座小塔，第五层上建主塔。

　　永燕塔主塔为钟形塔，大小塔的塔身敷金，基座涂白。盈江地区在公元 2011 年 3 月 10 日，遭遇 5.8 级地震，永燕塔遭到破坏，次年即已修复。永燕塔主塔的塔刹为宝伞。

　　Located on Yunyan Mountain east of Yingjiang County, Yongyan Pagoda was built in 1947 by the local headman Si Hongsheng to suppress water monsters, but, because of wars and plagues, was not completed until 1955.

　　The pagoda groups are composed of the main pagoda and 40 small pagodas. The main pagoda, with a square pedestal, is 20 meters in height and has five storeys tapering in width from the bottom up. On each side of the ground storey stand seven small pagodas. From the second storey and up, there is a small pagoda only at the corner of the storey. The main structure sits on the fifth storey.

The main building is in the shape of a hanging bell and the body of all pagodas is covered with gold, the pedestal colored in white. The pagodas were damaged because of an earthquake of 5.8–scale on March 10, 2011. The repair work had been done the next year.

The spire of the main building of Yongyan pagodas is in the shape of precious umbrella.

盈江永燕塔（邑石网供图）

香港聚星楼（魁星塔）

Tsui Sing Lau Pagoda Hong Kong

香港聚星楼（魁星塔）邮票（中国香港 1995 年发行）

香港聚星楼（魁星塔）邮票（中国香港 1980 年发行）

　　香港聚星楼又名魁星塔，当地人称为文塔。原址为新界原住民邓氏家族的风水塔。明洪武十五年（公元 1382 年），邓氏七世祖邓彦通在此建七级浮屠（佛塔），供奉文武诸神，"挡北煞，镇水妖"。魁星塔为六角形，用青砖和麻石砌筑，原为七层，遭飓风毁去四层，现存三层，这三层塔总高 13 米。各层正面皆有门楣题字，第一层为"光射斗垣"，第二层是"聚星楼"，第三层是"凌汉"。魁星塔塔刹今已不存。

　　The Tsui Sing Lau Pagoda, literally known as the Pagoda of Gathering Stars, is also called Wen Pagoda by Hong Kong residents. The original building is the geomantic pagoda owned by Deng families, locals of New Territories. It was built, in the year 1382 during the reign of the first emperor of Ming dynasty, by the seventh-generation ancestor, Tang Yin-tung, to avoid evil spirits from the north, prevent floods and help the Tangs win a title in the imperial examination.

Numerous Tangs have been granted titles. It was declared a monument on 14 December 2001.

The hexagonal, green-bricked building was originally seven-storey before a hurricane wiped away part of it. The residual three-storey structure stands 13 meters high. The door frames of the right sides of each storey have some inscriptions. The spire of The Tsui Sing Lau Pagoda is no longer in existence.

香港聚星楼（邑石网供图）

韩国佛国寺多宝塔

Tabo Pagoda Pulguk-sa R.O. Korea

（韩国 1979 年发行）佛国寺多宝塔邮票

（韩国 1978 年发行）佛国寺多宝塔邮票

  佛国寺多宝塔位于韩国庆尚北道庆州（在新罗时期此地称"徐罗伐"，公元935年高丽灭新罗后，始称庆州）。多宝塔是第20号韩国国宝，总高 10.4 米。

  多宝塔建于 756 年前后的新罗时期，全部用石材建造。

  佛国寺大殿之前有双塔，据记载是新罗时期国相金大城为纪念其父母而建。多宝塔第二层的四扇门之外，原先各有一只狮子。但在日本侵略者占领时期，其中三只已无踪影，现只剩一只。

  塔顶为多宝塔的塔刹，底层为刹座，上为仰莲、相轮、宝盖，再上为水烟，刹顶为双宝珠。

  Tabo Pagoda，also known as Dabotap is located in Gyeongju city of North Gyeongsang province，R.O. Korea. It totals 10.4 meters high and is currently designated as National Treasure No. 20.

The pagoda is supposed to have been built in about 756, the middle period of Silla. All parts of the pagoda are made out of stone.

There are two pagodas in front of the main hall of the temple of Bulguksa, which are recorded to have been built by Prime Minister Kim Daeseong to pacify the spirits of his parents.

There used to be a stone lion standing outside each of the four doors of the second storey, but three of them were lost during the time Japan formally annexed Korea. Currently, only one of the four stone lions survives.

The pagoda has a spire on top of it, the base of which is topped with blooming lotus petals, discs, canopy and water smoke. The spire top is in the shape of two precious beads.

佛国寺多宝塔(邑石网供图)

韩国佛国寺三层石塔

Three-storey Pagoda Pulguk-sa R.O. Korea

佛国寺三层石塔邮票（韩国1978年发行）

　　佛国寺三层石塔，也叫佛国寺释迦塔，位于韩国庆州，佛国寺大雄殿前方西侧，建于朝鲜半岛新罗时期，用石材建造。释迦塔是韩国第 21 号国宝。

　　释迦塔造型简洁，高 8.2 米。公元 1966 年 10 月在对释迦塔进行修复时发现塔内舍利洞内有一方形舍利函。

　　佛国寺释迦塔舍利函内有一卷用丝绸包裹的唐代雕版楮纸印本的《无垢净光大陀罗尼经》。舍利函内的经卷，经专家考证，该卷佛经是中国唐代初期在洛阳印刷的。尤为珍贵的是刊印佛经用的是唐朝楷体汉字，其中有若干中国 10 世纪以前民间通用的俗体字和异体字，这对研究汉字的发展和变迁有重要意义。

　　Three-storey Pagoda, also known as Seokgatap or Sakyamuni Pagoda, is located in Gyeongju city of North Gyeongsang province, R.O. Korea. It is on the

佛国寺三层石塔(邑石网供图)

left side in front of the main hall of the temple of Bulguksa. The stone pagoda is supposed to have been built during the Silla Period and is designated as National Treasure No.21.

The pagoda is of a very simple and basic design and stands 8.2 meters tall. A house—shaped sarira box was discovered inside the pagoda when the building was repaired in 1966.

Inside the sarira box, a copy of the Mugujeonggwang Great Dharani Sutra, wrapped up by a piece of silk, was found. It has been verified by researchers that the woodblock printing was made in Luoyang city at the early stage of Tang dynasty of China. What is notable is that the text of the print is written in Chinese handwriting of standard style of Tang dynasty, including many Chinese characters in popular form and variant forms, which is of great value to the study of evolution and changes of Chinese characters.

韩国塔坪里七层石塔

Seven-storey Pagoda Tappyeongri R.O. Korea

塔坪里七层石塔邮票(韩国1978年发行)

　　塔坪里七层石塔位于忠清北道忠州塔坪里，是韩国第 6 号国宝。

　　该塔建于新罗元圣王时期（约 8 世纪）。

　　塔坪里石塔高 14.5 米。由两层底座和七层塔身组成，石质塔檐由下而上逐层收分，造型优美。塔为方形，仿楼阁式。

　　塔刹较为特殊。有两层方箱两层宝盖，方箱之上为覆钵，刹顶为一方形莲花。塔身不见雕塑等文化信息。

　　Seven-storey Stone Pagoda is located in Tappyeongri near the Namhan River in North Chungcheong province，R.O. Korea and is designated as the 6th National Treasure. It is estimated to have been built during the reign of King Wonseong in the 8th century.

　　The stone pagoda is 14.5 meter tall and is comprised of a seven-storey body placed on a two-storey platform and a spire. The stone eaves diminish in size as they progress upward， which makes the building look very beautiful. The pagoda is square and in the shape of emulated pavilion.

The spire of the pagoda is in a unique style and departs considerably from those of typical stone pagodas of the Silla Period. It consists of a two–layer square platform topped with inverted bowl and two–layer canopy. The spire top is in the shape of square lotus petals. By contrast， the pagoda body carries no carvings and other cultural implications.

韩国弥勒寺石塔

Miruk-sa Temple Pagoda R.O. Korea

弥勒寺石塔邮票（韩国 1978 年发行）

弥勒寺石塔位于全罗北道益州市金马面箕阳里，是韩国第 11 号国宝，建于百济武王时期（公元 600—641 年）。该塔原为 9 层，后塔身倒塌，现尚存 6 层，高 14.24 米，且塔的半边已倒塌。

石塔在公元 1993 年修复，还原为九层石塔，塔高为 27.67 米。在公元 2001—2009 年修复过程中，出土金质琉璃壶、金质《舍利奉安记》等文物 500 余件。据《舍利奉安记》所载，此批文物是公元 639 年安放的。

Located in modern Iksan, North Jeolla province, R.O. Korea, Miruk-sa Temple Pagoda was constructed during the reign of King Mu of Baekje, who ruled from 600 to 641, and is designated as the National Treasure No.11. The pagoda originally has nine stories, but as a result of the building's collapse, only six storeys with a height of 14.24 meters survived.

The stone pagoda was restored in 1993 to its original nine-storey structure,

27.67 meters in height. During excavations in the years 2001–2009, more than five hundred historical relics were unearthed, including a gold pot and a gold plate with inscriptions in Classical Chinese on both sides. It is recorded that the relics were placed inside the pagoda in 639.

韩国芬皇寺石塔

Punhwang-sa Temple Pagoda R.O. Korea

芬皇寺石塔邮票（韩国 1978 年发行）

芬皇寺石塔位于庆尚北道庆州市九皇洞，是韩国第 30 号国宝。塔高 9.3 米，塔呈方形，现为三层。石塔是新罗时期善德女王于公元 634 年建造。

石塔是由黑色岩石磨成的砖块堆砌而成。据学者推测，石塔原为七层或者九层，塔刹已不见。佛塔底层四门的两侧，各有用汉白玉雕成的力士。黑色的塔身和白色的力士形成强烈对比。人们在塔内还找出舍利装置，证实是一座舍利塔。

Punhwang-sa Temple Pagoda is located in Gyeongju city of North Gyeongsang province，R.O. Korea，and is designated as National Treasure No. 30. The three-storey stone pagoda stands 9.3 meters tall and is square in shape. It is recorded to have been built in 634 under the auspices of Queen Seondeok of Silla.

The stone pagoda is made out of stones of black andesite cut like bricks. It is speculated by researchers that the pagoda originally stood nine stories tall with a spire at the top that is no longer extant.

Each side of the pagoda has what may have once been doors into the interior of the pagoda. Two figures guard each doorway and are known as Mighty Diamond Men. The black pagoda body and the white guardians form a strong contrast. The stone pagoda is proved to be a building for Buddhist relics, for sarira, or relic box were found inside the building.

韩国华严寺四狮子三层石塔

Four Lions Three-storey Stone Pagoda Hwaom-sa R.O. Korea

华严寺石塔邮票（韩国 1978 年发行）

　　华严寺四狮子三层石塔位于全罗南道求礼郡智异山山腰处，是韩国第 35 号国宝。佛塔是方形仿楼阁式塔。

　　佛塔建于新罗善德女王十四年（公元 645 年）。相传新罗善德女王执政时期，慈庄大师从大唐带回来佛舍利 74 块，为供养佛舍利而建此塔。现在的石塔是在公元 1636 年重建的。

　　华严寺佛塔的结构造型优美。塔基上建多层塔身，其中第二层有雌雄两对狮子，狮子中间有一合掌而立的僧人。第一层的四面，雕有天人、飞天、奏乐、鲜花等形象。塔身第三层雕有仁王像、四天王像、菩萨像等。

　　塔刹底层是宝匣，上面是宝盖，其上是覆钵，再上是相轮，刹顶是一颗硕大的宝珠。

　　Four Lions Three-storey Stone Pagoda is located on the slopes of Jirisan in the province of South Jeolla province，R.O. Korea and is designated as National

Treasure No. 35. The pagoda is square and in emulated pavilion-style.

The four Lion stone Pagoda was presumably erected in 645 under the auspices of Queen Seondeok of Silla. According to later accounts, Jajang was given some invaluable Buddha's sarira when he returned from China, so he constructed a pagoda to enshrine them. The extant building is a reconstruction of the pagoda made in 1636.

The Four Lion stone Pagoda is delicate in structure, composed of a two-layered platform and a multi-storey body. There are two pairs of statues of male and female lions standing at each corner of the platform's second layer. A Buddhist guardian deity surrounded by a thick rectangular border is engraved in low relief on each side of the body stone. These figures likely represent the Four Heavenly Kings.

The base of the spire is shaped as square platform, on which there are canopy, inverted-bowl and discs topped with a huge precious bead.

韩国贞惠寺十三层石塔

13-storey Pagoda Jeonghye-sa R.O. Korea

贞惠寺十三层石塔邮票（韩国 1978 年发行）

贞惠寺十三层石塔位于庆尚北道庆州市安康邑玉山里，是韩国第 40 号国宝。石塔建于统一新罗时期，高 5.9 米，为方形石塔。

实际上石塔是一座单层塔，十三层是塔刹的相轮。

贞惠寺石塔建在土石筑成的基础上，用四块石板组成地基，其上有四根石柱组成石塔的塔身。

塔身之上是塔刹，刹身是十三重相轮，塔刹刹顶已遗失。

Located in Gyeongju city of North Gyeongsang province，R.O. Korea，the 13-storey Pagoda was built in Silla Period and is designated as National Treasure No. 40. The square stone pagoda，standing 5.9 meters tall，is virtually a single-storey building. The thirteen-layered structure is the discs of its spire.

The stone pagoda rests on the earth and stone foundation，consisting of a stone base，a body made up of four stone pillars and a spire of thirteen-layered discs. The upper part of the spire is no longer extant.

韩国月精寺八面九层石塔

Octagonal Pagoda Wolchong-sa R.O. Korea

月精寺八面九层石塔邮票（韩国1978年发行）

　　月精寺八面九层石塔位于江原道平昌郡珍富面东山里，是韩国第 48 号国宝，塔高 15.2 米。佛塔是在高丽王朝时期（公元 918—1392 年）宣德王年间由慈藏律师修建的。

　　石塔有两层石质基座，上建九层石质密檐式塔身。石质塔檐由下而上逐层收分，塔身每层八个角都悬有风铃。

　　佛塔第一层的四周均辟小型佛龛，供奉佛像。

　　塔刹完整，底层为覆钵，上为仰莲，再上是相轮和宝盖。宝盖周边有放射状飞镖，宝盖之上为水烟，刹顶是两颗宝珠。

　　Located on Odaesan in Pyeongchang county, Gangwon province, R.O. Korea, Octagonal Pagoda was constructed by Jajang Yulsa, a celebrated Vinaya Master of the Goryeo Period（918—1392）. The building, 15.2 meters in height, is designated as National Treasure No. 48.

The nine-storey body of the stone pagoda, standing on a two-layer platform, is multi-eaved and made out of stone. The stone eaves diminish in size as they progress upward. Bells hang at eight corners of each storey. Small arched niches with statue of Buddha can be seen on four sides of the first storey.

The spire of the pagoda is complete in structure, consisting of a base shaped as inverted bowl, blooming lotus petals, seven-tiered discs, canopy, water smoke, and two precious beads at the top.

韩国景天寺十层石塔

Kyongch'on-sa Temple Pagoda R.O. Korea

景天寺十层石塔邮票（韩国 1978 年发行）

　　景天寺十层石塔是韩国第 86 号国宝。石塔原坐落在开城丰德郡，现迁至韩国国立中央博物馆。石塔建于高丽忠穆王四年（公元 1348 年）。该塔是由施主姜融和高龙凤特地从元朝选拔高级工匠来高丽建造的。建塔共用了 144 块在当地少见的大理石。每块大理石底部都刻有编号。景天寺石塔塔身下三层周边雕有狮子、罗汉，以及《西游记》中的场面，塔身还雕有栏杆、斗拱等。

Kyongch'on-sa Temple 10-storey Pagoda was constructed in 1348, Goryeo period and is designated as National Treasure No. 86. The stone pagoda was originally situated in Kaesong, but presently it has been relocated in National Museum of Korea.

The craftsmen who built the pagoda were chosen from China, Yuan dynasty. Totally 144 pieces of marble, rarely found in local area, were used for the construction and each marble is carefully numbered.

The pagoda is comprised of three parts, individually made and assembled afterwards. The base and the first three storeys of the body form the shape of Chinese character Ya, while the upper seven storeys are square in shape. The outer side of the first three storeys are carved with figures of lions and disciples of the Buddha and the designs of the story *Journey to the West*. Handrails and bucket arches are also made part of the pagoda body.

韩国阵田寺三层石塔

Three-storey Pagoda Jinjeon-sa R.O. Korea

阵田寺三层石塔邮票（韩国 1978 年发行）

　　韩国阵田寺三层石塔位于江原道襄阳郡屯田里，是韩国第122号国宝。阵田寺石塔建于统一新罗时期。石塔由道义大国师创建，道义大国师曾在公元784—821年入唐修学。

　　塔呈方形，底座两层，塔身三层，各层出檐较大。塔身和塔檐都是用整块石料雕琢而成。塔的两层基座都雕刻人物。底座下层雕天人像，每面有两人，上层雕八部神众护法像，每面两位，共八位。阵田寺三层石塔的塔身第一层高大，四面雕坐佛。

　　石塔的塔刹已残损，只余方箱和覆钵。

Located in Gangwon province, R.O. Korea, the three-storey Pagoda of Jinjeon-sa is designated as National Treasure No.122.

The stone pagoda was constructed in Silla Period under the proposal of a national master who used to study Buddhism in China during the years from 784

to 821.

The stone pagoda is square in shape, comprising a two-layered base and a three-storey body. The pagoda body and eaves are made out of the entire blocks of stone and the four sides of the first storey are caved with sitting Buddha. The two-layered base is also decorated with Buddhist figures. The spire of the pagoda is no longer complete in structure, only square platform and inverted bowl remaining.

朝鲜妙香山普照寺石塔

Pohyon Temple Pagoda D.P.R. Korea

妙香山普照寺石塔邮票（朝鲜 1986 年发行）

  妙香山普照寺石塔位于朝鲜平安北道香山郡，建于公元 1042 年（高丽王朝时期），塔高 10.03 米。是一座八角十三层石塔。佛塔在大雄殿之前。石塔十三层自下而上渐次收缩，各层形状相似，大小不一，宛如十三顶八角帽叠在一起。

  石塔下部有五层八角形石材基础，其上是十三层塔身，石塔各层八个角都挂有风铃。

  塔刹完好，底为八角座，上为相轮，再上为宝盖，宝盖之上为水烟，刹顶为双宝珠。

  Located in North Pyongan province，D.P.R. Korea，Pohyon Temple Pagoda was built in 1402，Goryeo period. Sitting in front of the Main Hall of the temple，the 13-storey stone pagoda is octagonal in shape，standing 10.03 meters tall. All the storeys of the building are similar in shape，decreasing in size as they progress upward, which makes the pagoda look like thirteen octagonal hats stacked.

At the bottom of the pagoda is the five-layered octagonal stone base, on which the main body is constructed. Bells hang at the eight corners of each storey. The spire of the building is well-preserved, comprising an octagonal pedestal, discs, canopy, and water smoke topped with two precious beads.

日本法隆寺五重塔

Horyu-ji Temple Pagoda Japan

法隆寺五重塔邮票（日本 1967 年发行）

　　法隆寺五重塔位于日本奈良，是日本国宝。它建于公元 607 年，塔高 32.45 米，佛塔为楼阁式，平面方形五层，纯木结构。

　　每层面积不大，层高也小，但挑檐很大，其中底层塔檐是重檐，是两层檐。整个塔看起来就像一只从天而降的大鹏鸟。

　　法隆寺五重塔的底层内部东西南北四面各有一组塑像。东面是文殊菩萨与维摩诘辩经；南面是释迦涅槃；西面是古印度国王散发舍利；北面塑像是佛家弟子。

　　法隆寺五重塔的塔刹十分华丽，塔刹高 9 米，塔刹底是宝匣，其上是覆钵，再上是九层相轮，相轮之上是水烟，再上是塔顶的两枚宝珠。相轮四周悬风铎。

　　法隆寺五重塔的塔中心有一中心柱，由地平直贯塔顶。塔内并无楼板，不能登临。

法隆寺五重塔（邑石网供图）

Horyu-ji Temple Pagoda is located in Nara, Japan and is designated as national treasure. Built in 607, the five-storey wood structure is square and pavilion-styled, standing 32.45 meters tall.

Each storey of the building is not large in size, neither is its height. By contrast, the eaves are very large, those of the first storey double-layered, which makes the pagoda looks like a big bird flying downward from the sky.

There is a group of statues on four sides of the first storey respectively, including the statues of Manjusri discussing with Vimalakirti about sutra, Nirrana of Sakyamuni, the king of ancient India distributing Buddhist relics and the Buddhist disciples.

The nine-meter-high spire of the wood pagoda is magnificent, with many components including square platform topped with inverted bowl, nine-tiered discs and water smoke. At the very top are two precious beads. Bells hang at every corner of the discs.

There are groups of statues of Buddhist figures inside the first storey of the pagoda. At the east side stands Manjusri talking with Vimalakirti, and south side Sakya, west side ancient Indian king distributing relics, north side Buddhist disciples.

日本室生寺五重塔
Murou-ji Temple Pagoda Japan

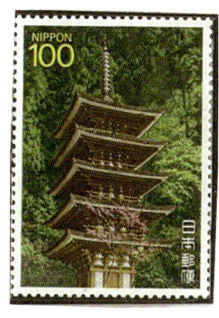

室生寺五重塔邮票（日本1988年发行）

　　室生寺五重塔位于奈良东北的室生村，建于公元 8 世纪。室生寺五重塔是日本国宝。塔身方形五层楼阁式，塔高 16 米，塔内供奉佛舍利。

　　室生寺五重塔依山而建，是日本最小的室外佛塔。据说佛塔是 8 世纪末僧人贤憬为祈求当时患病的皇太子早日康复而建。

　　该塔自下而上没有收分，各层大小相同，但挑檐很大。

　　该塔的部分结构，在公元 1998 年被台风吹毁，公元 2000 年修复。

　　室生寺五重塔塔刹完整，塔刹底为宝匣，上为覆钵、相轮、仰莲、覆钵、宝盖。刹顶为双宝珠。

　　Located in the northeast part of Nara, Japan, the Murou-ji Temple Pagoda was built around 800 and designated as national treasure. The square pagoda, with Buddhist relics enshrined inside, is 16 meters in height and in the style of pavilion. Built along the hillside, it is the smallest outdoor pagoda, and is allegedly constructed by a Buddhist monk to pray for the recovery of the sick crown prince.

The five storeys of the building are the same in size, each with huge overhanging eaves. In 1998, the pagoda was broken by a typhoon and was restored in 2000.

The spire of the five-storey Pagoda is relatively complete, with a base shaped like square platform topped with inverted bowl, discs, blooming lotus petals, canopy. Two precious beads are set at the very top.

日本药师寺东塔

Yakushi-ji Temple East Pagoda Japan

药师寺东塔邮票（日本 1976 年发行）

　　原塔建在藤原京，是天武天皇为了祈求皇后（即后来的持统天皇）身体健康而建。佛塔还未建成，天武天皇却不幸弃世，由持统天皇（即原天皇的皇后）自己继续修建，约公元 698 年建成。之后都城在公元 713 年迁至平城京（今奈良），寺塔也迁至此处。

　　药师寺东塔位于日本奈良市西京町，是日本国宝。塔身方形，楼阁式，纯木结构，塔高 37.9 米。

　　药师寺东塔结构特殊，塔身三层，大屋顶下又有小屋顶，和谐组合，看去像是六层。现塔底层尚有佛坛，供奉室町时代的四方佛和镰仓时代的四大天王像。

　　药师寺东塔的塔刹下为宝匣，上为相轮、水烟和双宝珠。

The pagoda was originally constructed in Fujiwara-kyo by Emperor Tenmu in the late 7th century for the recovery of the emperor's sick wife, who succeeded him as Empress Jito. After the death of Emperor Tenmu，his wife，Empress Jito，took over the job and completed the construction in 698. The temple and the pagoda were moved to Nara eight years after the Imperial Court settled in what was then the new capital.

The square wooden pagoda，standing 37.9 meters tall，is in the style of pavilion and is designated as national treasure. It has just three stories，but seems to have six because of the presence of inter-storey pent roofs．A butsudan still exists in the first storey，with Muromachi period statue of Buddha，and Kamakura period statues of Four Heavenly kings presented on it.

The spire of East Pagoda is in a common style，comprised of square platform at the bottom，discs，water smoke and two precious beads at the top.

日本药师寺东塔（图片左侧）与西塔（邑石网供图）

日本安乐寺八角三层塔

Anraku-ji Temple Octagonal Three-storey Pagoda Japan

安乐寺八角三层塔邮票（日本 1969 年发行）

　　安乐寺八角三层塔位于日本长野县上田市别所，为日本国宝。塔身八角三层，楼阁木塔。现塔建于公元 1288 年，高 18.75 米。

　　该塔原修建于"葛城寺"，建于 6 至 7 世纪。后来"葛城寺"衰败，该塔于公元 1288 年迁建至安乐寺，是日本现存唯一此类塔。从外形看像是四层塔，其实一、二层之间间距很小。

　　该塔是一座舍利塔，内藏佛祖的佛骨舍利及其他佛祖遗物。

　　安乐寺塔塔刹由宝匣、相轮、水烟和双宝珠组成。

Anrakuji Temple pagoda, designated as National Treasure, is located in Bessho Onsen, Ueda, Nagano Prefecture, Japan. The octagonal three-storey wooden structure built in 1288, is in pavilion style and stands 18.75 meters in height.

The pagoda was originally built in the 6th and 7th century inside Katsuragi

汉传佛教地区的佛塔

Temple and was moved to Anrakuji Temple after the decay of Katsuragi Temple. It is the only extant octagonal pagoda in Japan.

The pagoda is a building for Buddhist relics, keeping inside the relics and other remains of Buddha.

The spire of the pagoda is comprised of square platform, discs, water smoke and two precious beads.

日本金刚三味院多宝塔
Kongo Sanmi-in Tahoto Japan

金刚三味院多宝塔邮票（日本 1988 年发行）

金刚三味院多宝塔位于高野山小田原谷，是日本国宝。塔身方形，楼阁式、纯木结构。建于公元 1223 年，高 14.9 米。

据说是在公元 1211—1223 年间尼将军北条政子为了祭奠其丈夫和儿子而捐资修建的，塔内供奉五尊佛像，还藏有"极彩色"（日本的一种绘画技巧）的佛画。

多宝塔塔刹完整。底为宝匣，上为覆钵、仰莲、相轮，再上为宝盖、仰莲、水烟和双宝珠。

Kongo Sanmi-in Tahoto, designated as national treasure, is located in Kongō Sanmai-in, Mt. Kōya, Japan. The square wooden pagoda, constructed in 1223, is a pavilion-style structure and stands 14.9 meters in height.

The construction of the pagoda is said to be sponsored by a famous Japanese political woman in honor of her husband and son. The building houses five statues of Buddha and many Buddhist pictures created with Japanese drawing techniques.

The spire of the pagoda is complete in structure, with a base in the shape of square platform topped with inverted bowl, blooming lotus petals, discs, canopy and water smoke. Two precious beads are set at the very top.

越南顺化天姥寺塔
Thien Mu Temple Pagoda Vietnam

（越南1990年发行）
越南天姥寺塔邮票

（南越1958年发行）
越南天姥寺塔邮票

越南天姥寺塔又名福缘塔，位于越南顺化，建于公元1844年。

阮朝嘉隆皇帝为庆皇后80大寿而建，初名慈仁塔。天姥寺塔高21.27米，是一座七层八角楼阁式塔，是顺化市标志性建筑。以福缘塔为主要建筑的天姥寺是世界文化遗产。

天姥寺塔是一座典型的楼阁式塔，属于北传佛教系统的一座佛塔。天姥寺塔每层正面供奉一座佛像，每层还有一副汉语对联。

天姥寺塔面临莲花潭，此潭与香江相通，塔身倒映潭中。波光塔影，景色绮丽。

Thien Mu Pagoda, also known as Linh Mu Pagoda, is located in the city of Hue in Vietnam. The pagoda was constructed in 1844 under the order of Hoang, the governor of Hue, to celebrate the 80th birthday of his wife.

The octagonal seven-storey building, 21.27 meters in height, is the most

汉传佛教地区的佛塔

recognizable landmark of Hue. The temple where the pagoda stands is listed as a site of World Cultural Heritage.

As one of the pagodas in northern Buddhism areas，it is a structure of typical pavilion-style. The front side of each storey is dedicated to a statue of Buddha，and in addition，a couplet of Chinese characters is presented in each storey.

Facing lotus pond leading to Perfume River，the pagoda has an inverted reflection in the water of the pond，which，together with the surrounding，forms a very beautiful scenery.

天姥寺塔（邑石网供图）

藏传佛教
地区的佛塔
Pagodas in Tibetan Buddhism Areas

北京北海白塔
Beihai Park White Pagoda Beijing

北海白塔邮票（東埔寨 1999 年发行）

　　北京北海白塔位于北京北海公园琼华岛上，建于清顺治八年（公元1651 年）。北海白塔塔高 35.9 米，是一座喇嘛式佛塔，是为迎接五世达赖喇嘛进京而修建的。

　　康熙十八年（公元 1679 年）北京地震，白塔损坏严重，康熙二十年（公元 1681 年）重建。雍正八年（公元 1730 年）北京又遭地震，这次再建，雍正十一年（公元 1733 年）完工。

　　北海白塔由塔基、塔身和塔刹三部分组成。塔基分为两层基台，一层基座。第一层基台，面积1650平方米，其上为第二层基台，面积1165平方米。再向其上为方形基座，是一高大的十字折角形须弥座，面积588平方米。基台和基座的立面是素面砌砖。

第二层基台周边建有汉白玉栏杆。在其上除了建有须弥座，在塔前面，还建有叫"善因殿"的琉璃小殿。

白塔须弥座之上是塔身。塔身正面辟"焰光门"。门内有一幅红底金字的藏文图案，据说是"吉祥如意"的意思。

1976年唐山大地震，波及北京，白塔受损。维修时在刹顶意外发现金质舍利盒，内藏佛舍利，证明白塔是一座舍利塔。

塔身之上是塔刹。塔刹底座是正方形十字折角形须弥座，座上是十三重相轮，相轮内有一根柏木刹杆，长约30米。相轮之上是宝盖，宝盖有天盘和地盘两层，上为天盘，直径约3米，重约1500公斤。地盘更大，重约2000公斤。宝盖之上是仰月，仰月之上是太阳，最上面是火焰宝珠。地盘周边挂有16颗铜铃。

北海白塔（朱静阳摄影）

Located on Qionghua Island, Beihai Park of Beijing, Beihai White pagoda was built in 1651 during the reign of Shunzhi Emperor of Qing dynasty. It is 35.9 meters tall and is typical of Lamaist pagodas. The pagoda was first constructed to honor the visit of the 5th Dalai Lama in 1651.

The pagoda was badly damaged by an earthquake in 1679 during the reign of Kangxi Emperor and was restored two years later. It was hit again by another earthquake during the reign of Yongzheng Emperor. The reconstruction took about three years.

Beihai White pagoda is composed of three parts: the base, the body and the spire. The base consists of a two-layer platform and a pedestal. The first layer of platform covers an area of 1650 square meters, on which is the second layer of 1165 square meters. A large square Sumeru pedestal, with an area of 588 square meters, sits on the two-layer platform. The four sides of both platform and pedestal are paved with bricks without any design.

The second layer of the platform is surrounded with white marble balustrades. Beside the Sumeru pedestal on the platform, a small temple, known as Shanyin Temple, is erected in front of the pagoda.

On the Sumeru pedestal is the pagoda body, with a door on its right side. The wall inside the door is decorated with a few Tibetan words in gold color against the red background, meaning "Good Luck and Happiness".

The White Pagoda was damaged again in 1976 because of the Tangshan earthquake near Beijing. As it was restored, a reliquary containing relics of Buddha, secreted inside the spire top, was found, which shows that the white pagoda is a pagoda for Buddhist relics.

The spire is on the main body of the pagoda. At the bottom of the spire is the square Sumeru pedestal, topped with the 13-layer discs in which there is a 30-meter-long wooden pole. The canopy on the discs has two layers. The upper layer is three meters in diameter and weighs 1500 kilograms. The lower layer is bigger weighing about 2000 kilograms with sixteen bronze bells hanging from it. Atop the canopy are components including the crescent moon, the sun and the flame-shaped precious bead.

北京妙应寺白塔

Miaoying Temple White Pagoda Beijing

（尼泊尔 2005 年发行）

北京妙应寺白塔邮票

（柬埔寨 1999 年发行）

北京妙应寺白塔邮票

　　北京妙应寺白塔位于北京妙应寺内。建于元至元十六年（公元 1279 年），原在寺名为"大圣寿万安寺"。明初（公元 1368 年），遭火焚，寺庙尽毁，白塔幸存。明宣德八年（公元 1434 年），寺庙修复，改称"妙应寺"。

　　白塔由塔基、塔身和塔刹三部分组成。塔基分三层，最下层为正方形，上、中两层为亚字形须弥座。塔基上砌覆莲，覆莲之上有五条环带，承托塔身，白塔由尼泊尔工匠阿尼哥设计建造，是一座典型的喇嘛塔。妙应寺白塔高 50.9 米，底座面积 1422 平方米，塔身最大直径 18.4 米。

　　塔刹底部是亚字形须弥座，其上是十三重相轮，意为十三天。 其上为直径 9.7 米的华盖。华盖以木作底，上置铜瓦，并做成 40 条放射形的筒脊，华盖周边挂 36 副铜质透雕的流苏和风铃。刹顶为小型喇嘛塔，有八条铁链将宝顶固定在华盖铜盘之上。

　　公元 1978 年，在对白塔的维修过程中，在宝顶中发现清乾隆十八年（公元 1753 年）留存的佛像、佛经等文物。其中有《大藏经》、乾隆手书《波罗蜜多心经》、木雕观音像和赤金舍利长寿佛。

妙应寺白塔（朱静阳摄影）

White Pagoda is located at Miaoying Temple in the West District of Beijing. The temple, originally known as Wan'an Temple, was built in 1279 and was ruined as a result of fire in 1368, early Ming dynasty. Fortunately, the pagoda survived. The temple was restored in 1434 during the reign of Xuande Emperor of Ming dynasty and renamed as Miaoying Temple.

The Pagoda is composed of three parts: the base, the body and the spire. The base covers an area of 1422 square meters and consists of three layers. The lowest layer is square-shaped and on the upper layer is seated the polygonal angle cross Sumeru pedestal. There is a huge lotus-flower-leave-shape construction built on the pagoda foundation to support the pagoda body. The white pagoda, a typical Lamaist building, was designed and constructed under the supervision of a Nepalese architect Arniko. The pagoda is 50.9 meters high, the main body of which is 18.4 meters in the maximum diameter.

At the bottom of the spire is the polygonal angle cross Sumeru pedestal, on which there are, 13-layered discs called "Thirteen Heavens". Further up is the canopy, 9.7 meters in diameter, which has a wooden baseplate covered with copper tiles. 36 pierced copper plates and copper bells hang down around the canopy. A small Lamaist pagoda is seated on top of the spire fixed to the copper plates by eight iron chains.

Some priceless Buddhist treasures were discovered when the Pagoda was being renovated in 1978, including the statue of Buddha kept in the 18th year during the reign of Qianlong Emperor of Qing dynasty and Buddhist scriptures such as *Tripitaka* and *The Heart Sutra* transcribed by Qianlong Emperor, wood-carved statue of Avalokitesvara and fine gold Buddha.

山西五台舍利塔

Wutai Sarira Pagoda Shanxi Province

五台舍利塔邮票（中国 1997 年发行）

　　五台舍利塔位于五台山台怀镇，俗称白塔。通高 75.3 米，是一座喇嘛式塔。舍利塔初建于元大德五年（公元 1302 年），是由尼泊尔工匠阿尼哥设计建造，全部用石头筑成。

　　明成祖永乐五年（公元 1407 年）曾重修此塔，工程浩大。到明万历七年（公元 1579 年）再次维修，据万历七年（公元 1579 年）敕建大宝塔记曰："基至黄泉，高二十一丈，围二十五丈，状如藻瓶，上十三级，宝瓶高一丈六尺，镀金为饰，覆盘围七丈一尺，吊以垂带，悬以金铃。更造金银宝玉等像化，造像书经，如云而集，悉纳藏中，十年壬午秋，工成。及诸杂宝安置藏中，海内皇宗宰官，士庶沙门，景仰慈并及寺宇佛殿经楼藏轮禅室，罔不备焉。"可见当时之盛况。

　　现塔为一座喇嘛式白塔。塔的最下层是塔台，塔台是方形，高 1.5 米，周长 126 米，四角建四个小亭。在其上建八角形塔座，塔座高 3.5 米。塔座上是两重八角束腰须弥座，再往上就是上大下小的圆形塔身。

　　塔身下层建三间佛殿，俗称塔殿，殿内供奉释迦佛像和文殊、观音、普贤及地藏菩萨。塔座南面有三个低而浅的石洞，右边洞内有"佛足碑"。据传万历年间重修白塔时，少林寺和尚翻祖前来献佛足图，即命刻碑立于此。塔座北面也有小洞，洞内供韦陀像。

塔身之上是塔刹。塔刹先是八角束腰须弥座，其上是十三重相轮，相轮上是宝盖。宝盖是一大型圆形平盘，周长 23.1 米，由八块铜板拼合而成。圆盘边缘吊装 36 块铜板，每块铜板长 2 米多，宽近 1 米，每块铜板下挂三只风铃。宝盖之上是小型喇嘛塔，喇嘛塔之上是风磨铜宝瓶。

Located at Mount Wutai of Taihuai county, Shanxi province, Sarira Pagoda, also known as The Great White Pagoda, was first built under the supervision of a Nepalese architect Arniko in 1302 during the reign of Dade

五台舍利塔（邑石网供图）

Emperor of Yuan dynasty. The stone pagoda with a height of 75.3 meters is a Lamaist building.

A large-scale reconstruction was made in 1407 during Ming dynasty, and a repair was made in 1579 during the reign of Emperor Wanli of Ming dynasty. The construction of the pagoda was recorded on a stone tablet dating back to 1579 during the reign of Emperor Wanli. According to the inscription, the construction was the greatest scale of work at the time and the huge pagoda looked magnificent and housed a lot of precious statues and scriptures.

The residual white pagoda is a Lamaist pagoda. The lowest part of the base is the square platform which is 1.5 meters tall and 126 meters in perimeter. Four small pavilions are erected at four corners around it. A 3.5-meter-high octagonal pedestal sits atop the platform and further up is a two-layered octagonal sumeru pedestal supporting the round body of the pagoda, the upper part of which is larger than its lower part.

There are three halls built in the lower section of the pagoda body, where statues of Shakyamuni, Manjusri, Bodhisattva, Samantabhadra and Ksitigarbha are enshrined. Three low and shallow holes can be seen on the southern side of the base, and inside a hole on the right side there is a tablet of Buddha footprint which is said to be installed during the reign of Emperor Wanli when the pagoda was renovated. The hole on the northern side is installed with the statue of Bodhisattva Wei Tuo.

The spire on top of the pagoda body is comprised of an octagonal sumeru pedestal, 13-layer discs, and a canopy. The canopy, composed of eight copper plates, is a large round plate with a perimeter of 23.1 meters. 36 pierced copper plates, each 2 meters long and 1 meter wide, hang down around the canopy. On the canopy is a small Lamaist pagoda topped with a copper precious bottle.

藏传佛教地区的佛塔

图书在版编目（CIP）数据

邮票上的佛塔 / 陈德芬编著；陈莉翻译.—西安：
西北大学出版社，2018.7
　　ISBN 978-7-5604-4210-5

　　Ⅰ.①邮…　Ⅱ.①陈…②陈…　Ⅲ.①邮票—世界—
图集②佛塔—介绍—世界　Ⅳ.①G262.2-64②K917.5

　　中国版本图书馆CIP数据核字 (2018) 第 176387 号

邮票上的佛塔

编　　著：	陈德芬
英文翻译：	陈　莉
出版发行：	西北大学出版社
地　　址：	西安市太白北路229号
邮　　编：	710069
电　　话：	029-88303059
经　　销：	全国新华书店
印　　装：	陕西隆昌印刷有限公司
开　　本：	787毫米×1092毫米　1/16
印　　张：	12.5
字　　数：	192千字
版　　次：	2018年7月第1版　2018年7月第1次印刷
书　　号：	ISBN 978-7-5604-4210-5
定　　价：	68.00元